# Power BI Step-by-Step
# Part 3: Power Query, Parameters, Templates & Custom Functions

*Hands-on Tutorials*

*By*

*Grant Gamble*

*for*

*G Com Solutions IT Training*

Copyright © 2018

gcomsolutions.com

# Contents

# Introduction

Welcome to this series of short eBooks on Microsoft Power BI. This series aims to provide hands-on training on all the different nooks and crannies of this exciting new product. In this third book in the series, we focus on using the Query Editor to perform data cleansing and transformation.

The first thing that you will need to do is to download the exercise files which are required to complete the step-by-step tutorials. To do this, visit the following link:

http://bit.ly/pbsbs3

aka:

https://gcomsolutions.co.uk/downloads/pbi_step_by_step_3.zip

(N.B. Underscore character used in URL.)

Once you've downloaded and unzipped the exercise files for this course, it is probably a good idea to delete the ZIP file, just to avoid confusion.

Next, head to the unzipped exercise folder, and here you will find everything that you need to complete the tutorials in this book.

# Chapter 1: Power BI Dataflows vs Power BI Desktop

Power BI now offers two environments in which to use Power Query to perform data connection, cleansing and transformation: using the Query Editor in Power BI Desktop; and using Power BI Dataflows, in app workspaces, in the Power BI service.

The Query Editor is Power BI Desktop's built-in Power Query tool for connecting to data sources and carrying out ETL (extract, transform, load) operations. Since, Power BI Desktop runs locally on each user's computer, it is almost inevitable that some duplication of effort will occur in most organizations; as different users connect to the same data sources.

Power BI's new dataflows allow the centralization of data cleansing and transformation operations, greatly reducing inconsistencies and duplication of effort across organizations. Instead of connecting to data sources from within a Power BI Desktop PBIX file, organizations will now be able to carry out all their Power Query data connection and transformation centrally in the Power BI service.

Since each dataflow must be created inside of a specific app workspace, the only real way to centralize their use is to create an app workspace (or several if necessary) dedicated to storing dataflows and not designed to be published as an app. Report creators can then be given member access to these dataflow-only app workspaces.

Centralization of data can then be achieved simply by ensuring that all report creators base their reports on dataflows. That way, for each new report created, if a suitable dataflow already exists, it can simply be used; if one does not exist, it can be created and reused in the future.

The following diagram shows how two dataflows might be used to centralize reports created for a manufacturing and sales department, using on-premises data sources. The diagram shows two types of app workspaces: dataflow and content. However, these types are created purely by organizational design; in reality, there is only one type of app workspace in Power BI.

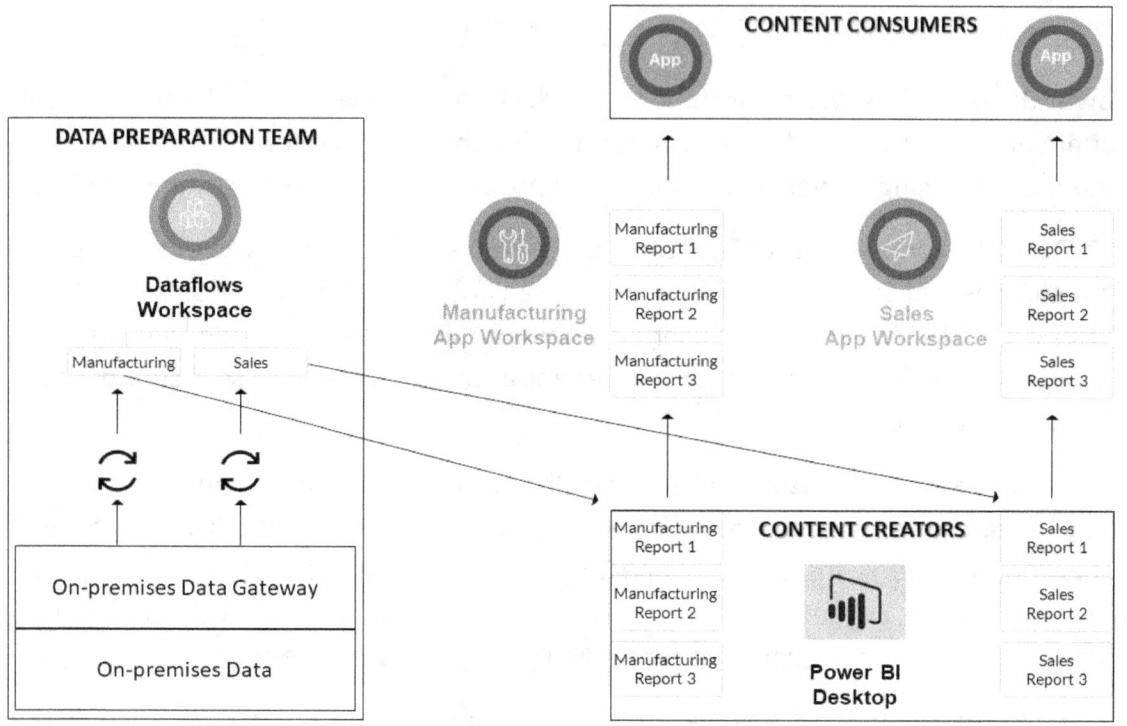

By design, an organization can decide that dataflow workspaces will contain only dataflows: no dashboards, reports, workbooks, or datasets. Since they contain no reports or dashboards, this means that these app workspaces can never be published as apps; either deliberately or accidentally.

Let's look at how we might create a sales report, working within the framework shown in the diagram above. Let's say that our organization uses a departmental model in creating app workspaces: one for each organizational department. Thus, we already have a "Sales" app workspace. And let's also say that we have a workspace called "Organizational Dataflows", in which we plan to create all our dataflows, and nothing else. Finally, let's assume that we have an on-premises data gateway installed and configured.

## Data Preparation

Firstly, a member of our preparation team creates a Sales data flow inside the "Organizational Dataflows" app workspace, using the key steps shown below.

In the Power BI service, click Workspaces > Organizational Dataflows > Dataflows.

Click Create > Dataflow.

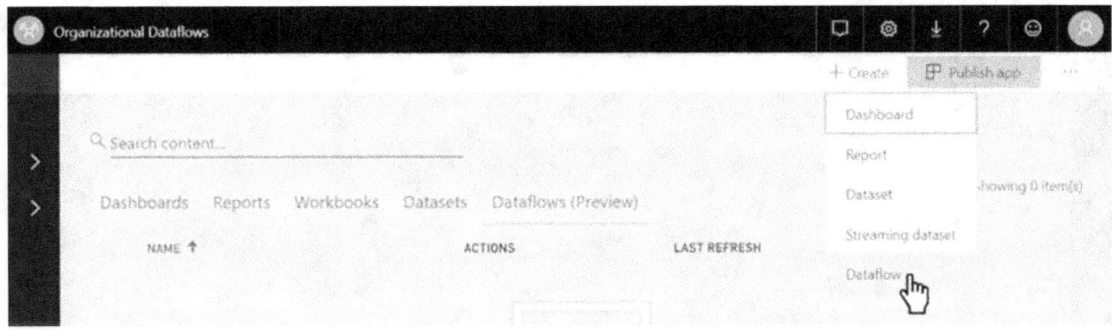

This creates a new, unsaved dataflow. Next, click on the **Add New Entities** button. (An entity is any element within an organization about which one needs to store data. Each entity will be represented as a table within the data model.)

You will then be given access to all the data sources to which you can connect. All the data sources available within Power BI Desktop will eventually be available as data sources for Power BI dataflows.

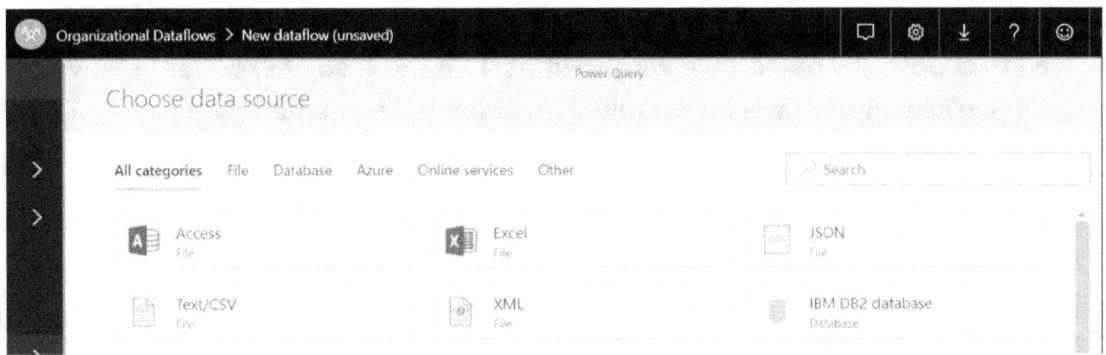

In this example, we will use Excel as our data source. When we click the Excel button, the Power Query Connection Settings screen appears; and, since the Excel file is stored on a local drive, we are forced to choose an on-premises gateway and enter our credentials.

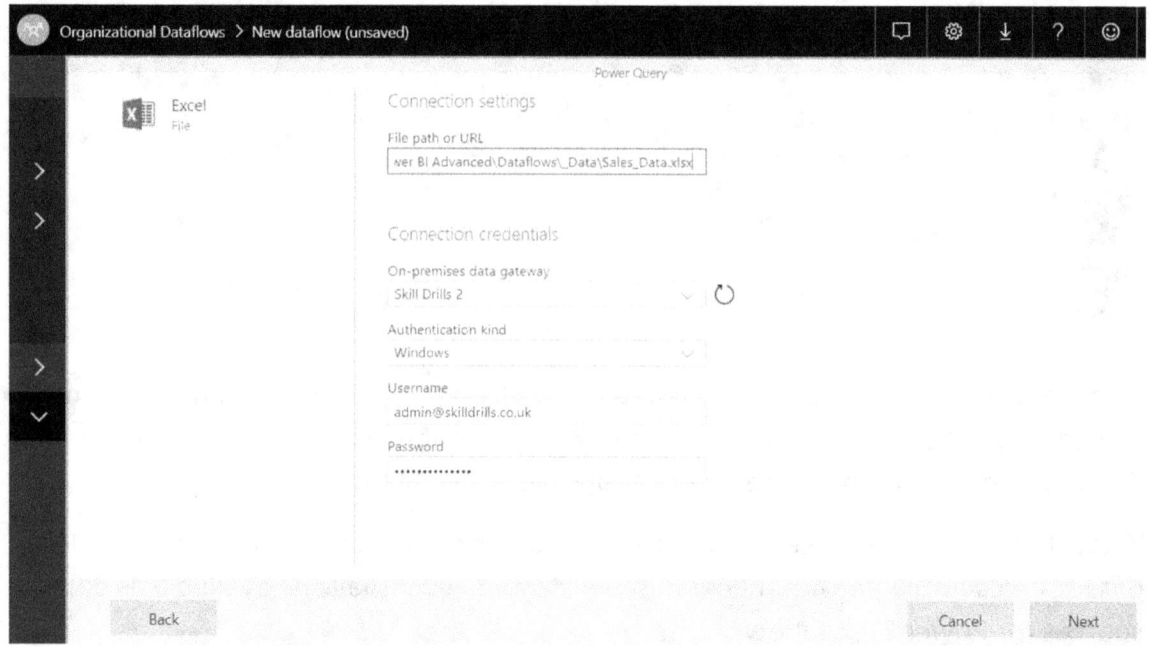

When we click the Next button, we are given a preview of the available data and allowed to choose the objects we wish to import. In the case of Excel, as in Power BI Desktop, we can import data from tables, worksheets and named ranges.

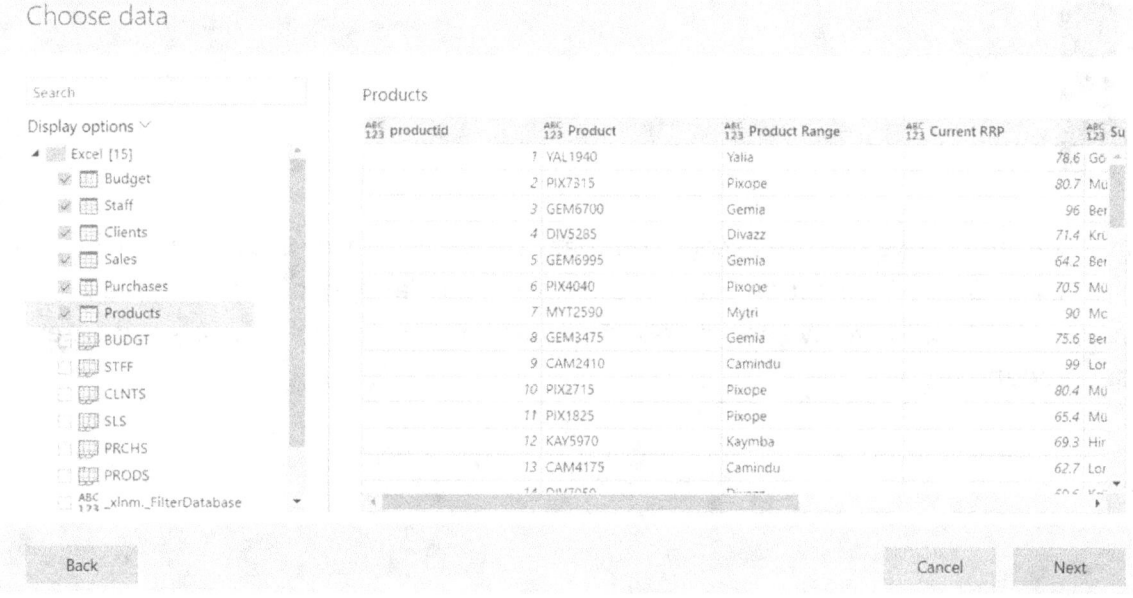

Clicking the Next button takes us into the online Query Editor which we can assume will be functionally identical to the Power BI Desktop Query Editor when the product is fully developed.

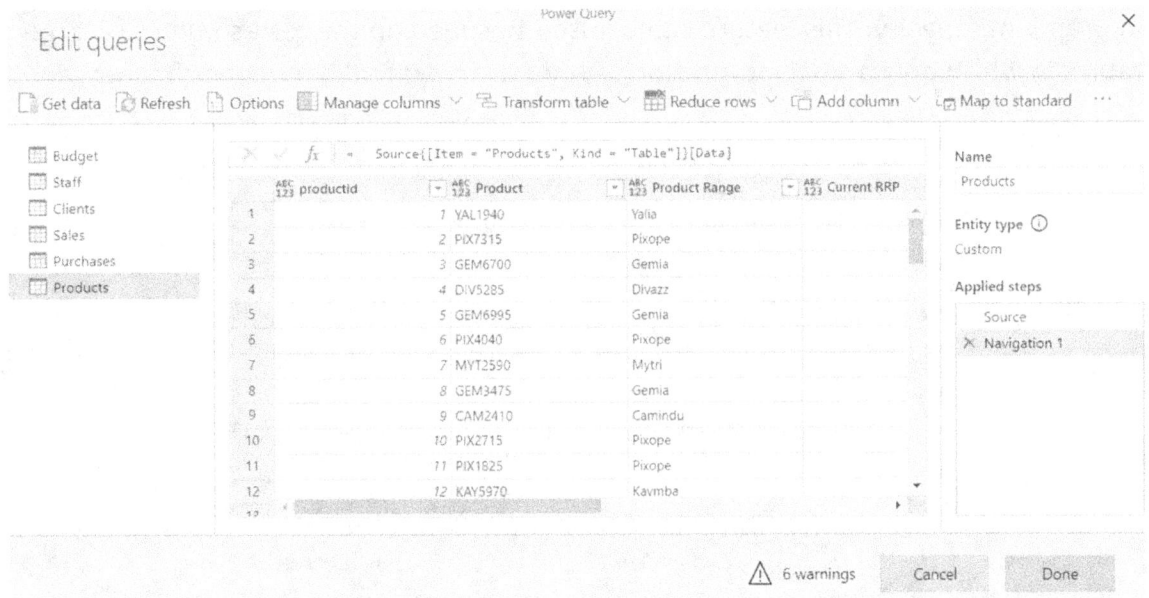

Here, we perform our data cleansing and transformation using a combination of visual commands and M language coding. When we are finished and click the Done button, we are presented with a list of all the entities we have created.

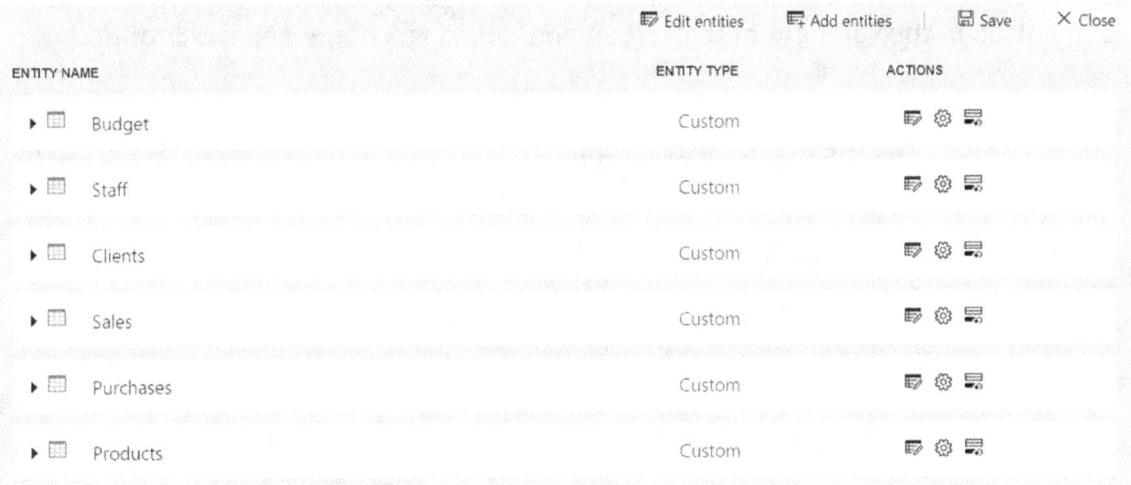

On the right of the name of each entity, we have three Action buttons: Edit Entity, Properties and Incremental Refresh. The Edit Entities button allows you to re-enter the Query Editor and make further changes. The Properties button allows you to enter metadata about the dataflow, such as a description.

The Incremental Refresh button allows you to force the refresh of an individual entity (the feature works at the entity, not the dataflow, level). It requires that the entity contain a datetime field and that the app workspace containing the dataflow is in premium capacity. This feature can be used to speed up the refresh times of large tables in which only a small proportion of rows are modified between refreshes.

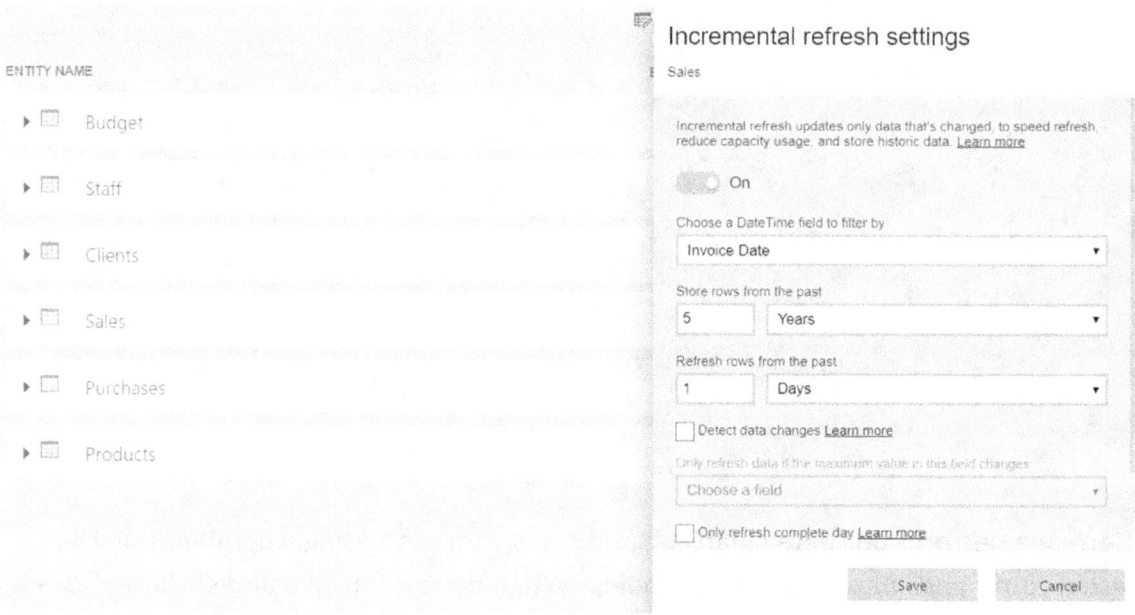

The final step is to save all the changes you have made to the dataflow by clicking the Save button in the top right of the screen and entering a name and description.

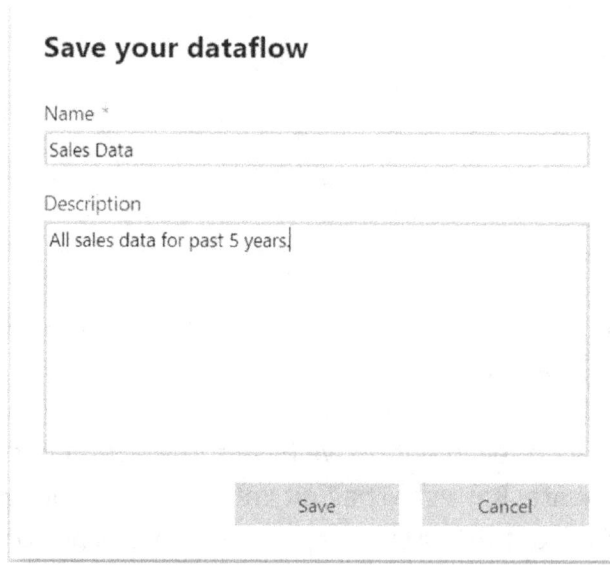

If the dataflow contains on-premises data, you will be given the opportunity of setting a refresh schedule using the on-premises data gateway.

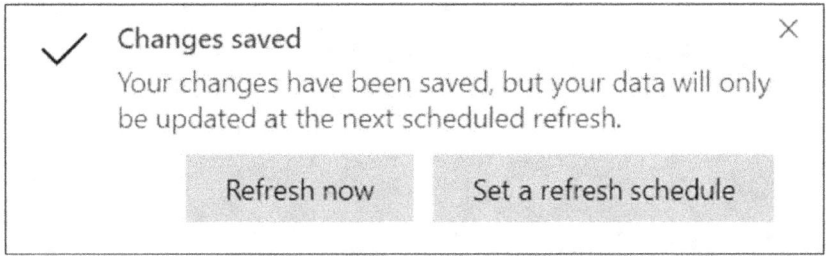

You can also perform this step manually at any time by clicking on Settings (the cog icon) > Settings > Dataflows and activating the Scheduled Refresh option.

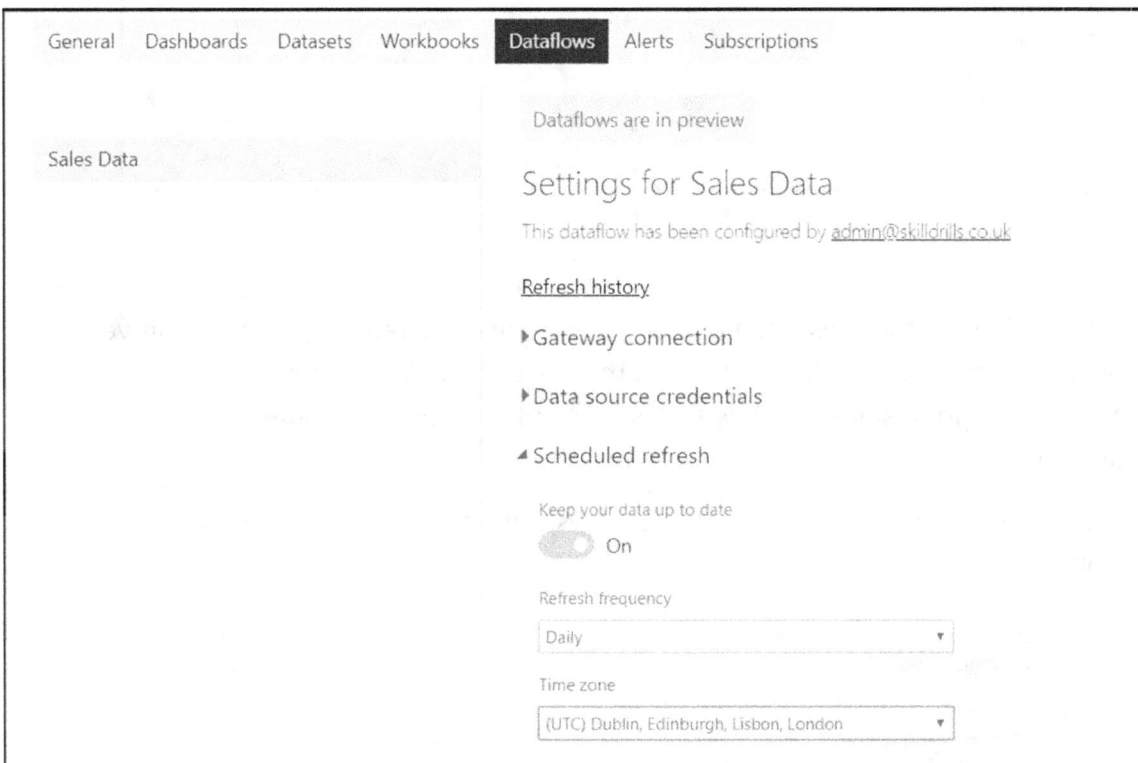

In a Power BI Pro capacity app workspace, you can schedule up to 8 refreshes per day; if the app workspace is in premium capacity, you can schedule up to 48 refreshes per day.

## Using a Dataflow as a Data Source

In Power BI Desktop, this dataflow can now be used repeatedly, as a definitive data source when building sales reports. At the time of writing, Power BI Desktop is the only viable option since the Power BI service offers no data modelling or DAX capabilities.

Click Home > Get Data > Power BI dataflows; sign in, if necessary; and click the Connect button.

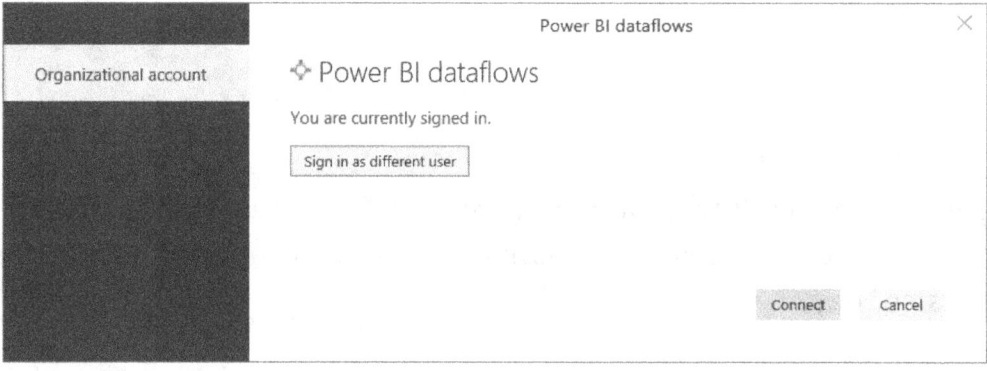

Unlike the experience of connecting to a Power BI dataset, connecting to a Power BI dataflow is not an all-or-nothing experience. You can specify the entities to which you want to connect.

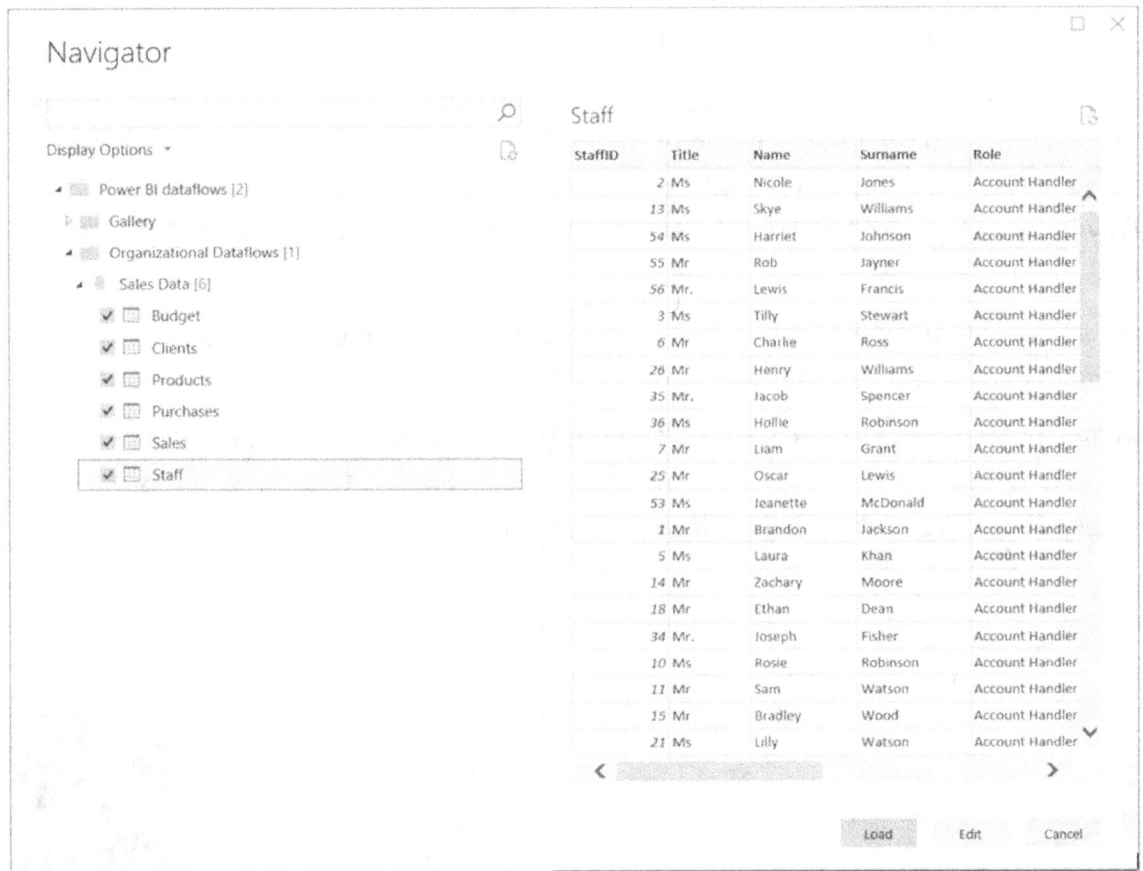

You can also connect to additional data sources within the same report and perform data modelling operations as normal.

## Conclusion

Although Power BI dataflows provide a useful mechanism for standardizing data preparation, they do have some disadvantages.

For example, to get the most out of dataflows, you need to invest in Power BI Premium.

Features such as incremental refresh (whereby only data that has been changed is actually refreshed) are only available in Premium workspaces. Additionally, since dataflow entities are stored as CSV files, they preclude the option of direct query connections to database servers.

For the rest of this book, we will be using Power BI Desktop as our connection and transformation tool. However, bear in mind that most of these operations can also be performed in the cloud when creating dataflows.

# Chapter 2: Trim, Clean and Case

When you are connecting to data, it is almost always the case that you need to make modifications to the data as it comes in and this is where the Query Editor becomes very useful. In this section we will focus on working in the Query Editor and on using its very user-friendly but powerful tools to transform the data that you are bringing in to Power BI.

Let us begin with an example which will be fairly familiar to Excel users; the need to remove extra spaces from columns of data to avoid errors and discrepancies.

In Power BI Desktop, let us **Home > Get Data > Text/CSV**. In sub-folder "02-Trim Clean and Case", let us bring in the file Trim-and-clean.csv. Then, to work in the Query Editor, we click on **Edit** as opposed to Load.

I will also just remind you how you exit the Query Editor and how we re-enter it. Click on **File > Close & Apply** and this takes us out of the Query Editor and back to Power BI Desktop. Then, to get back into the Query Editor at any time, chose **Edit Queries** from the Home Tab of the Ribbon.

So, in the Query Editor, we have this very rich, very powerful environment at our disposal; and we will begin our look at the Query Editor, with some very useful, clean up functions. If you look at the Name column, in the imported query, you can see that we have a problem with spaces. We can see that there are spaces preceding some entries; we can also assume that there will be spaces following entries on certain rows; and we also have some extra spaces between words.

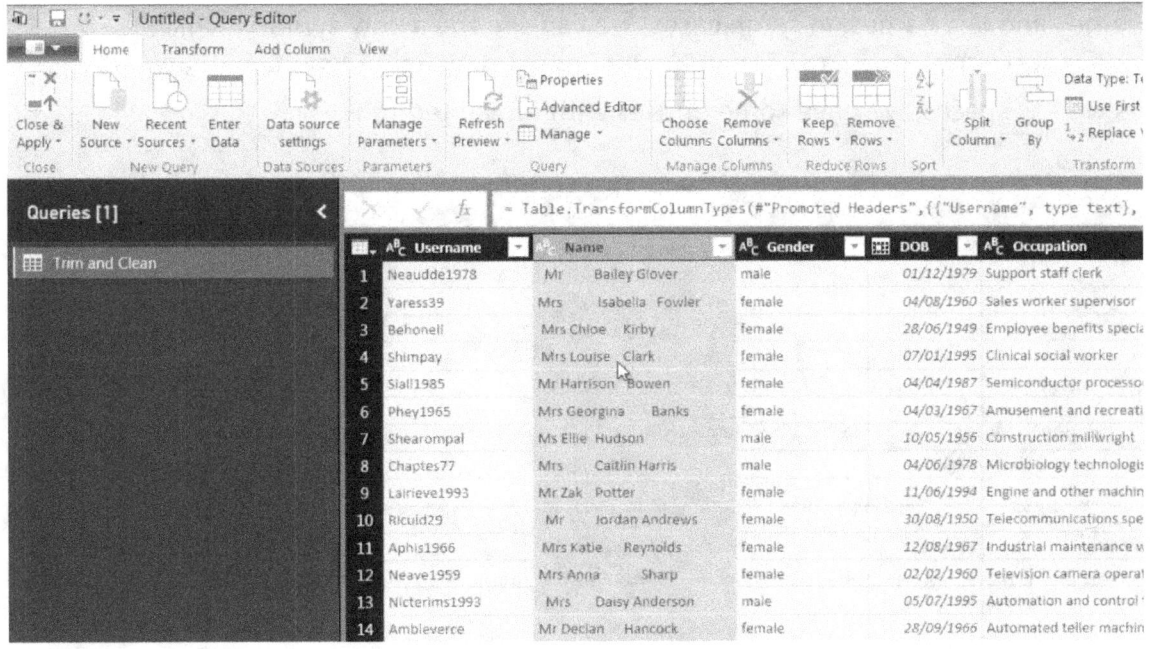

## Isolating the Problem

When looking to clean up text it is always useful to know what you are looking for; and one way of doing this might be to open the text file in Microsoft Word and then try and review the invisible characters. As well as opening the CSV, we can also copy the entire table from the drop-down menu in the top left of the table, and then just paste the copied data into Microsoft Word.

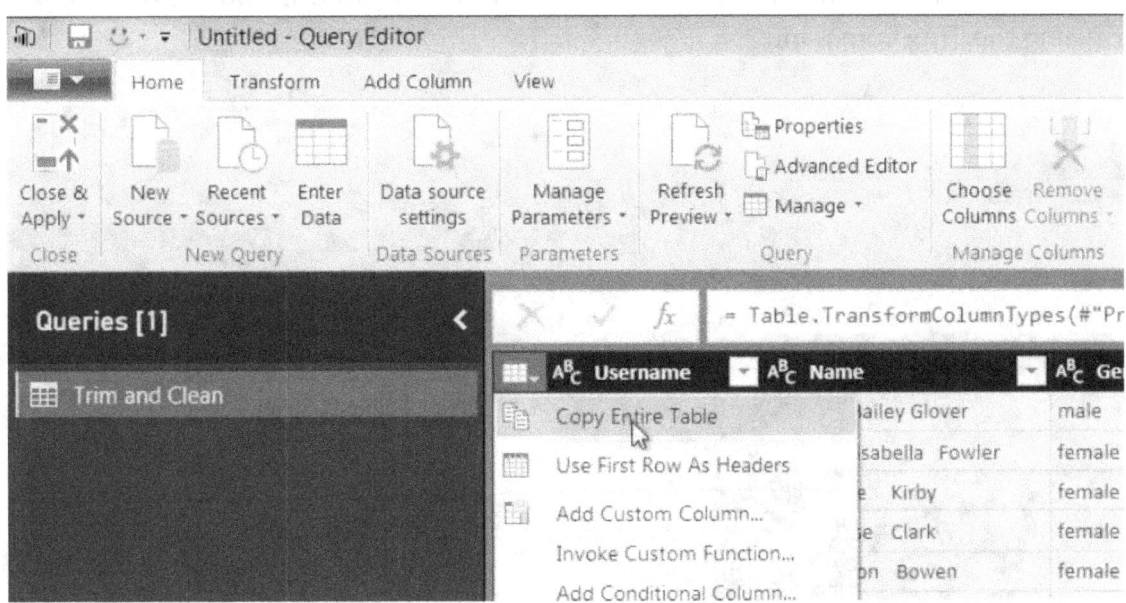

Once the data is pasted into Microsoft Word, using the Show Paragraph Marks feature, we can see some examples of what is going on between some of the first names and last names. In some cases, we can see the arrow symbol, which represents a Tab character. (The tiny dots represent spaces.) So, we now know that, as well as spaces, we have some entries with unwanted tabs.

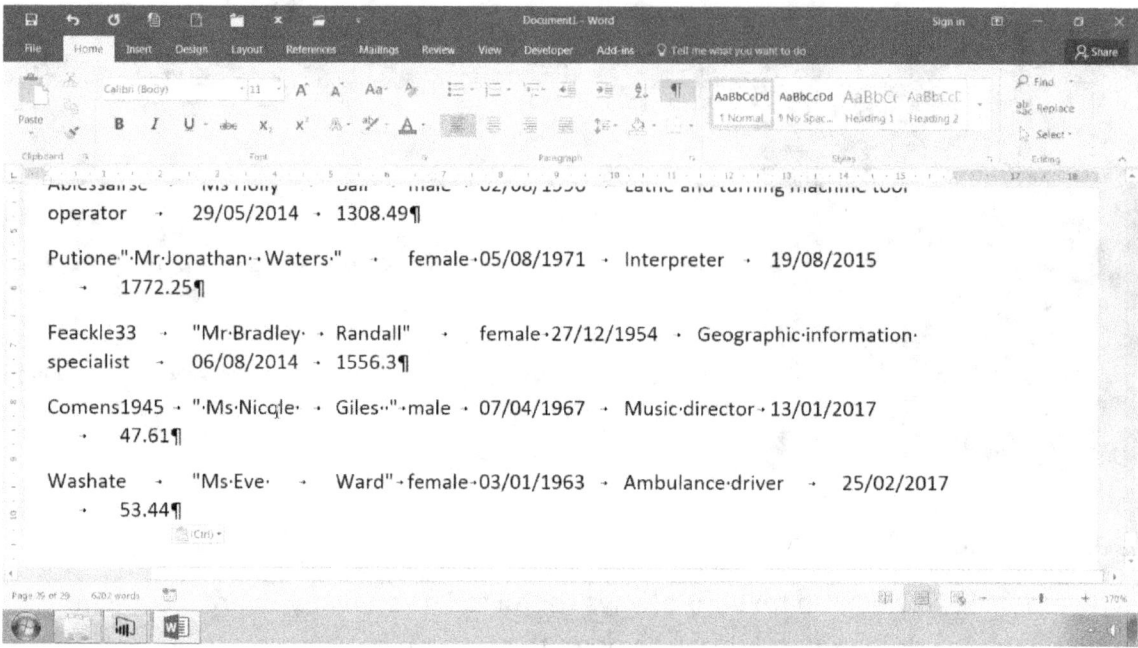

## Using the Trim Function

Back in the Power BI Query Editor, we begin by highlighting the Name column and activating the Transform Tab, where we will find the **Format** drop-down. Let us begin by using the Trim command.

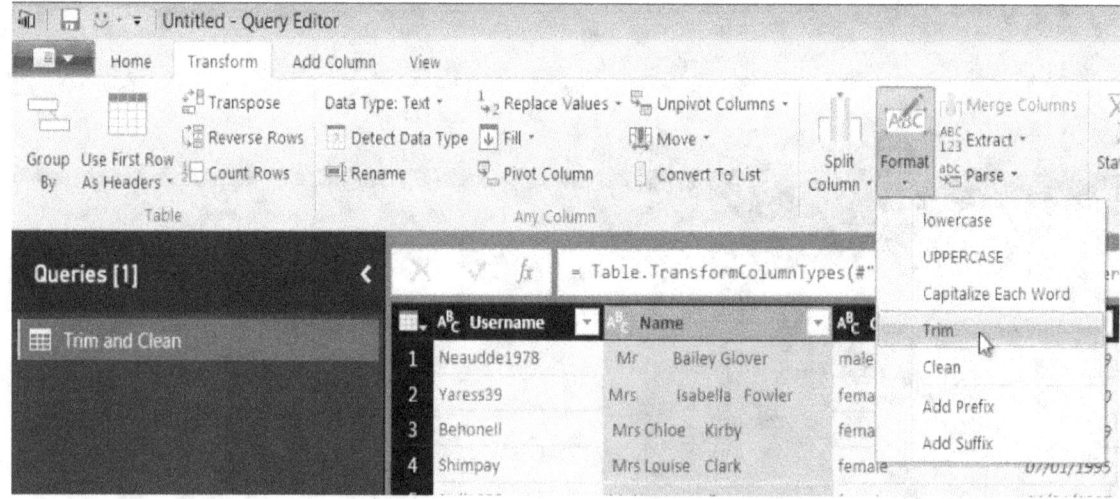

You may well have come across Excel's version of this function; the Query Editor command is very similar; it removes the leading and trialling spaces; but it does not have any effect on the spaces between words – a key difference between the M version and Excel's offering.

## Using the Clean Function

In Microsoft Word, we spotted a tab between some of the first name and last name combinations. To remove characters like tabs and returns from text entries, in **Transform > Format**, you chose **Clean**. You will see that this operation has removed a lot of extra spacing; and we can now assume that any remaining extra spaces are simply multiple occurrences of the space character.

## Using the Replace Values Command

We can, therefore, use the **Transform > Replace Values** command to remove any remaining characters.

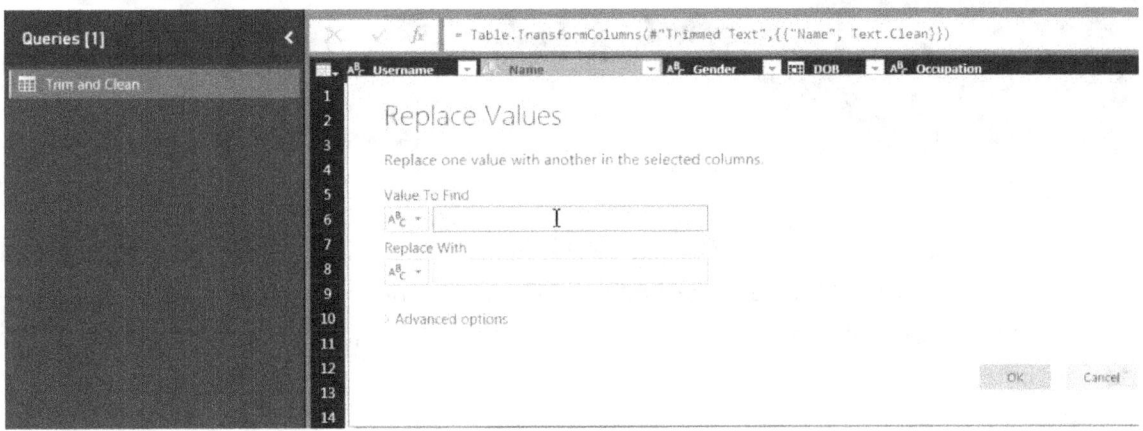

Let us assume that three spaces are the maximum we need to think about; so, firstly, we replace three spaces with one. If our guess is correct, then two spaces will be the maximum remaining. This time we replace two spaces with a single space.

Now, if we look at the steps we have performed, as shown in the Applied Steps pane; we have had to perform four steps to get rid of the space that we have identified; and this is typical when cleaning up data and preparing it for use in the data model.

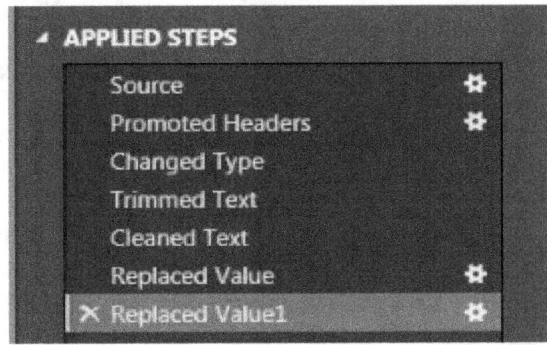

## Using the Capitalize Each Word Command

We will finish our first look at the Query Editor by modifying the gender column. Let us say we do not like lower case for this column and would prefer title case; with the first letter capitalised.

In the same place as Clean and Trim, i.e., **Transform > Format**, you will find the options for changing case; **lowercase** and **UPPERCASE**; and title case is obtained with the option **Capitalise Each Word**.

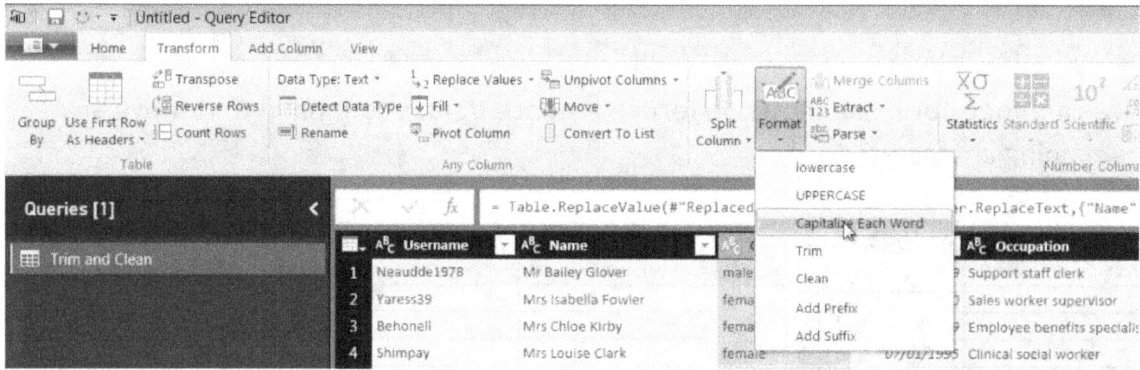

## Conclusion

This concludes our first look at cleaning up data. In the next chapter, we will look at housekeeping, renaming items and adding metadata to clarify what steps you are performing.

# Chapter 3: House Keeping and Meta Data

Let us continue our look at the Query Editor by examining a few important housekeeping features which it is useful to get into the habit of using. In the exercises folder, open the folder "03-Renaming and adding metadata". Here you will find a single PBIX file: "Renaming.pbix". Double-click to open this file.

This is the file that we were working on in the last chapter. To get back into the Query Editor let us click on **Edit** Queries and chose **Edit** Queries from the drop down. This is almost certainly what you will see.

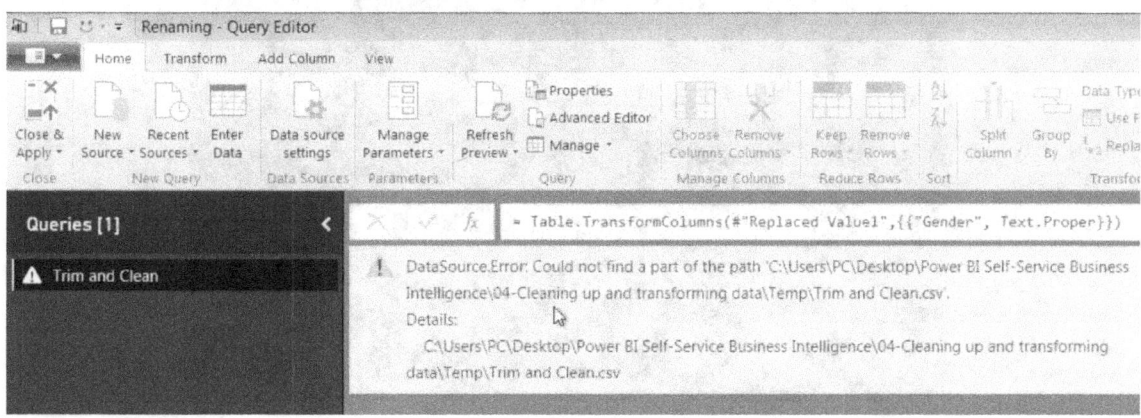

This is simply an indication that, when the file was created, a text file was imported from a specific path; and, on the current system, the file is no longer available at this same specified path.

It is very easy to cure this problem. We go back to the source step and click on the settings icon (the cog).

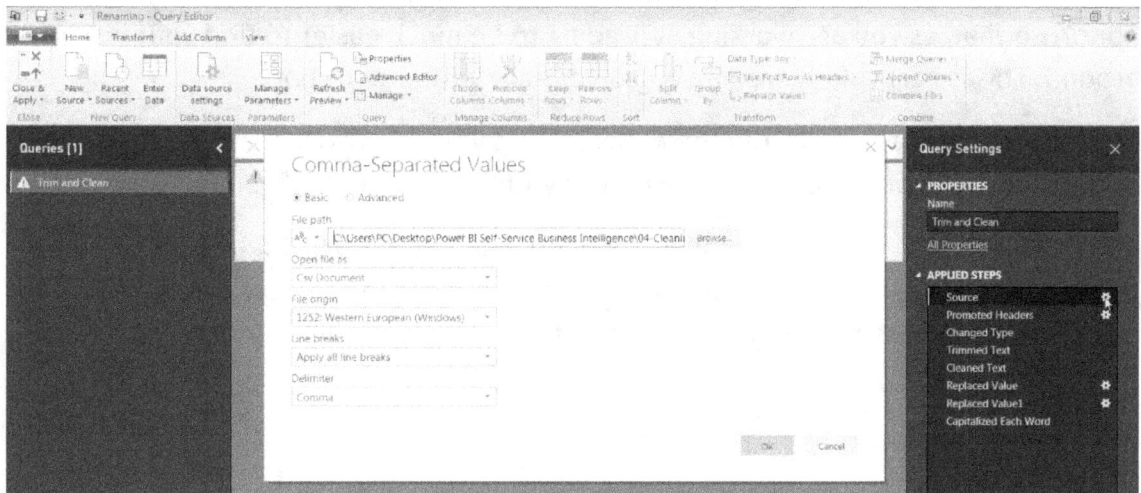

Then, we enter the current location of the file we wish to import: "02-Trim, Clean and Case\Trim-and-clean.csv". You will probably find it quicker to copy and paste the folder path that precedes the filename. Once you do this and click **OK**, the error will disappear. Then we can see the final query that we created, and we can see the final step in the Applied Steps pane.

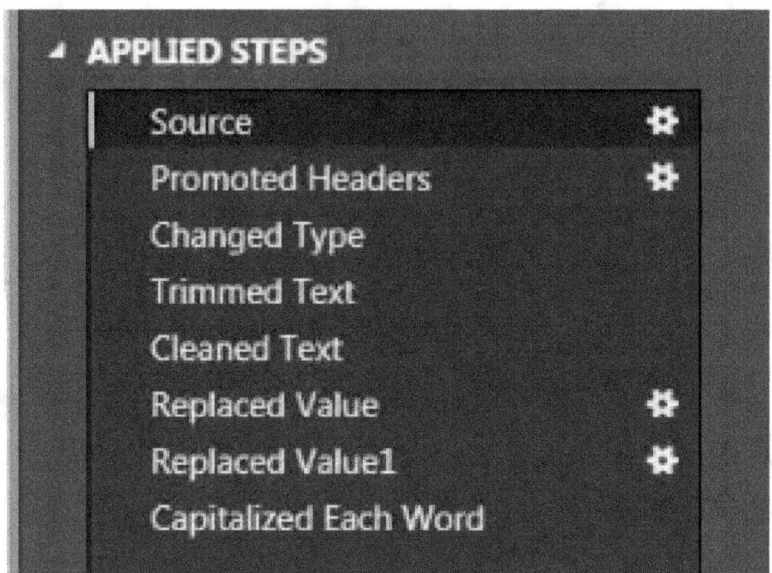

Let's now review some of the housekeeping steps that we can employ to add clarity to our Power Query workflows.

## Renaming Items

When building a report, you will typically require several queries; and, with each of these queries, you'll need to perform a series of transformational steps. If you get into the habit of renaming items, this will help to add some clarity to the Query Editor; so that, as you are working, it is going to be much easier to find your way around. This is particularly true if you collaborate with other people.

Renaming items helps to clarify the datasets that you are working and gives you an opportunity to replace code-friendly names with human-readable ones.

The first thing that we can rename is the query itself, to do this, **Right-click** on the query, and choose **Rename**. (You may also be aware of the shortcut; this is the standard Windows shortcut for renaming a file: simply press F2.)

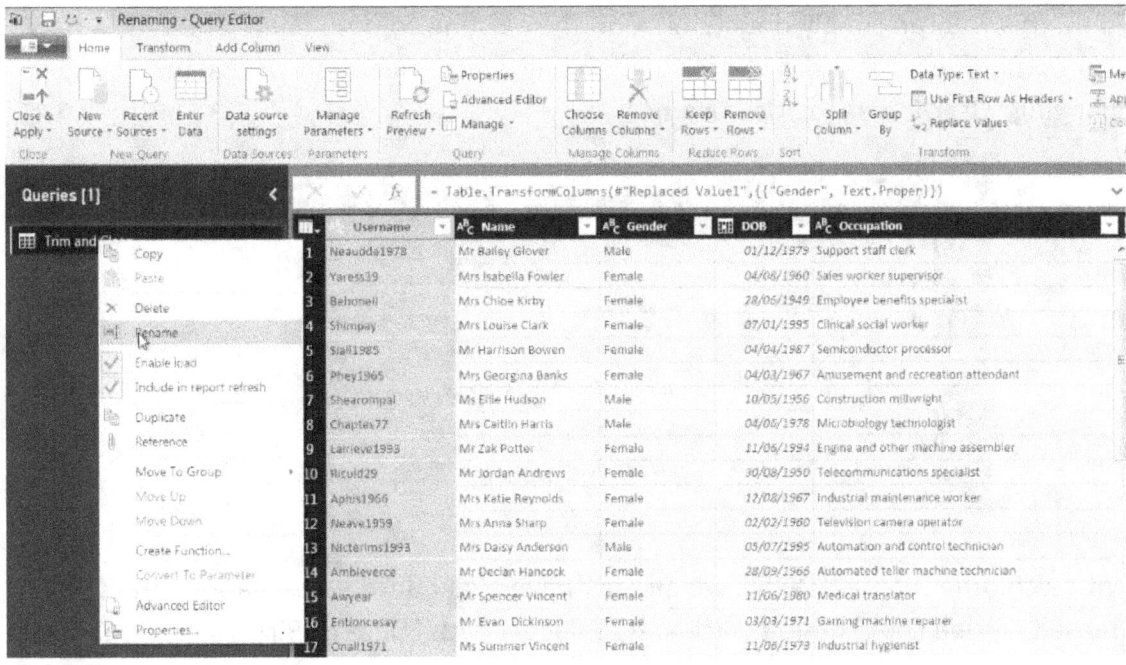

This dataset is a list of subscribers, so let us rename the query "Subscribers" and press enter. We can achieve the same result in the Properties pane; right at the top, we have a Name field which we can also modify.

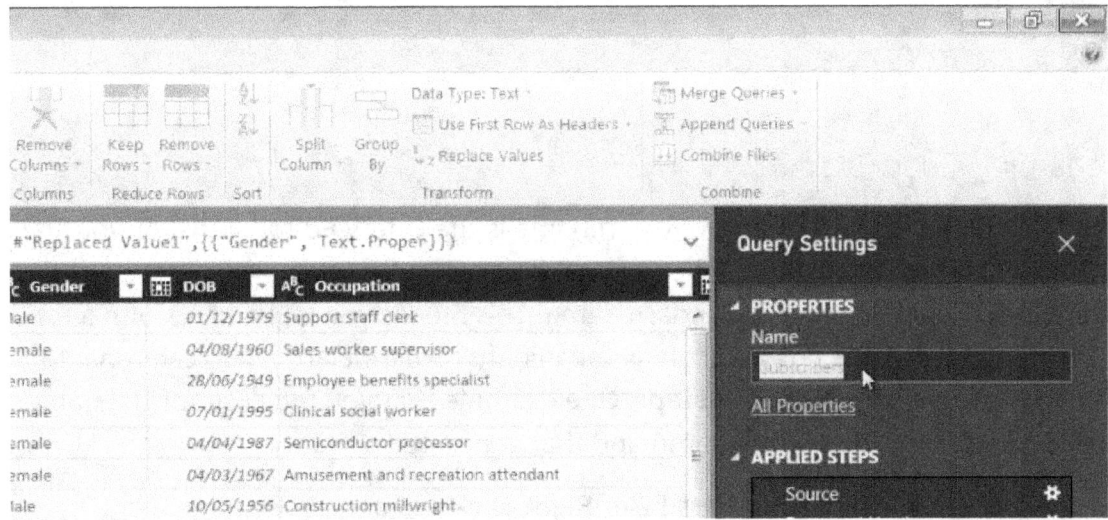

## Renaming Columns

The next thing which it is a good idea to get into the habit of changing is the names of your columns. As you build reports, the field names will be displayed on category axes, tooltips, headers, etc; and the consumers of your reports will be exposed to these names. So, if you use cryptic, system-friendly names rather than user-friendly ones, it is a good idea to get into the habit of renaming your columns.

To do this you can simply double-click on the existing column name and type a new one. Sometimes, it is just a matter of inserting spaces between words; for example, changing "Username" to "User Name".

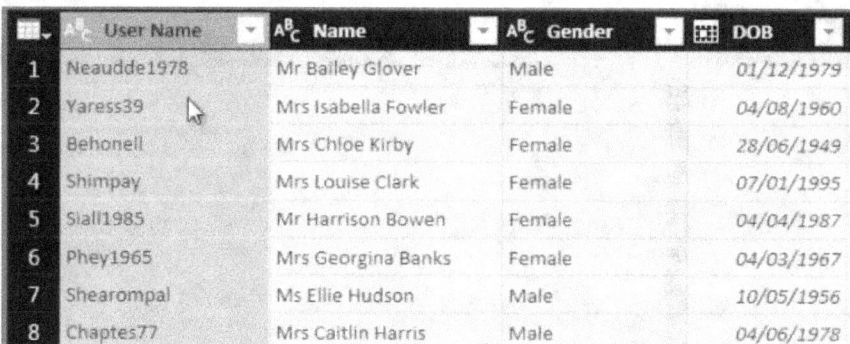

With a column such as "DOB", we already have a standard abbreviation; but if you wanted to, you could double-click and replace it with "Date of Birth".

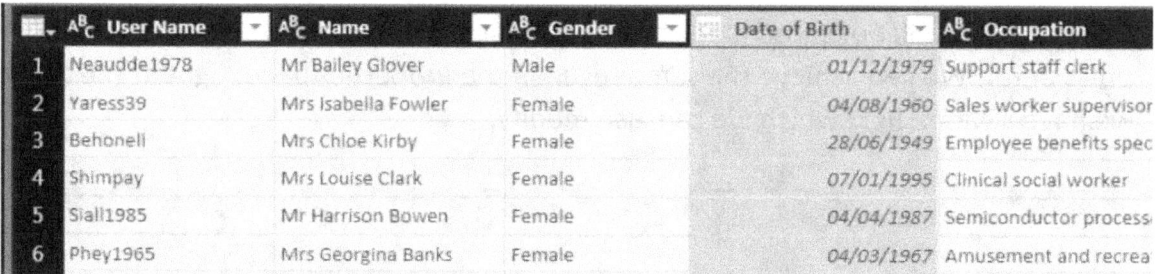

## Renaming Query Steps

The third type of element that we can rename is the Query Editor steps. As you perform your transformations, the Query Editor will automatically generate a series of steps and give each one a standard name. This means you will end up with a lot of similar names that are not particularly meaningful. So, for clarity, you can rename these fields just like in previous steps. One example that you may use for the name of a step is the location of the command that generated it.

Again, it is possible to either press F2 or **Right-click** and choose Rename. For example, we could rename the "Trimmed Text" step "Transform/Format/Trim"; to remind other users of the location of the command that was used to create that step.

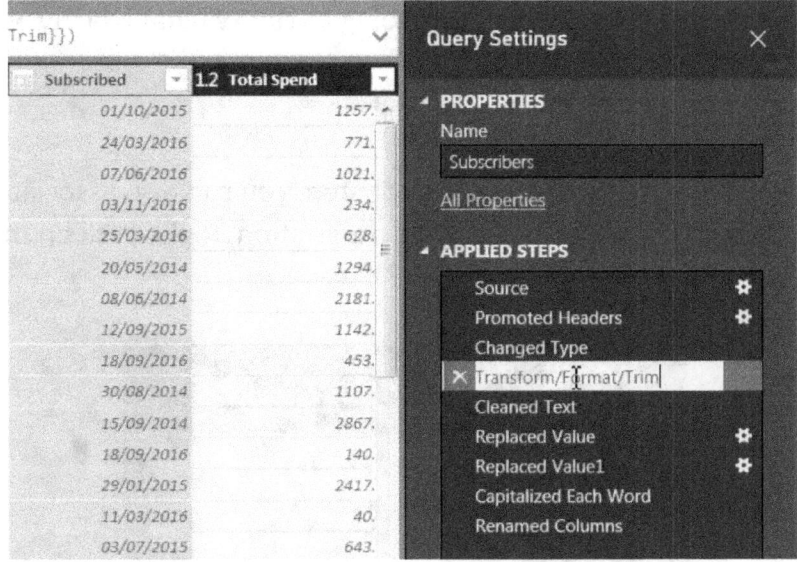

In a similar way, we could change "Cleaned Text" to "Transform/Format/Clean".

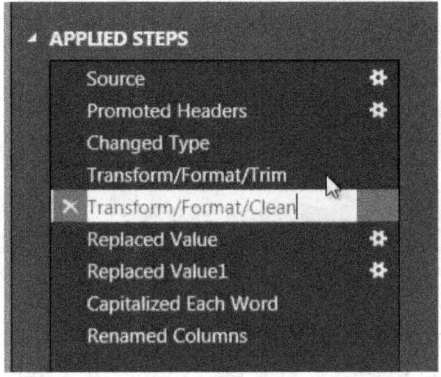

Then we have a couple of "Replaced Value" steps. Here, we could simply specify the text before and after. Thus, we could change "Replace Value" to "3 spaces -> 1" and "Replace Value1" to "2 spaces -> 1".

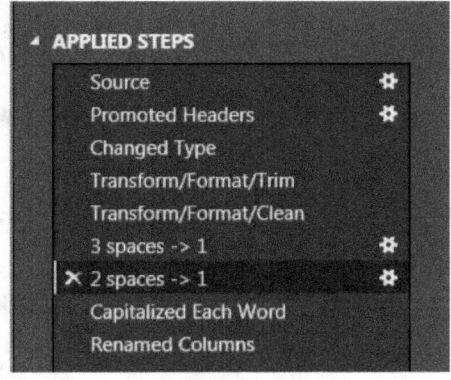

I'm sure you get the idea; anything that is going to clarify what exactly went on in each of these steps.

## Adding Descriptions to your Steps

As well as changing the name of Query Editor step, you can also associate a description with each of the steps. To add a description, **Right-click** on the step and select Properties.

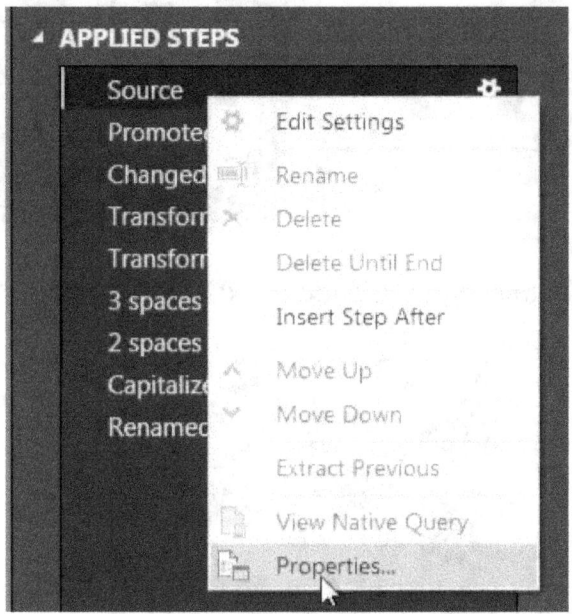

Here, you have a chance to enter some metadata. For clarity, and for the benefit of anyone else working on this project, you can describe each key step; why it is important; and why it needed to be done.

So, for example, on our first step, we might enter: "Automatically applied by Query Editor".

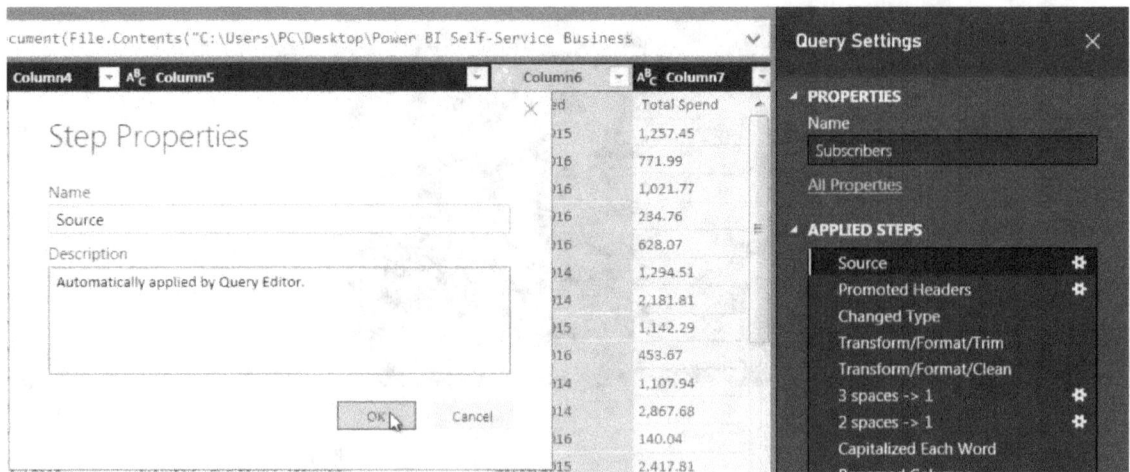

And we could copy this same text and use it for the next two steps.

Then, moving onto the Trim step, we could enter: "Step 1 of 4 for removing unwanted spaces in name column".

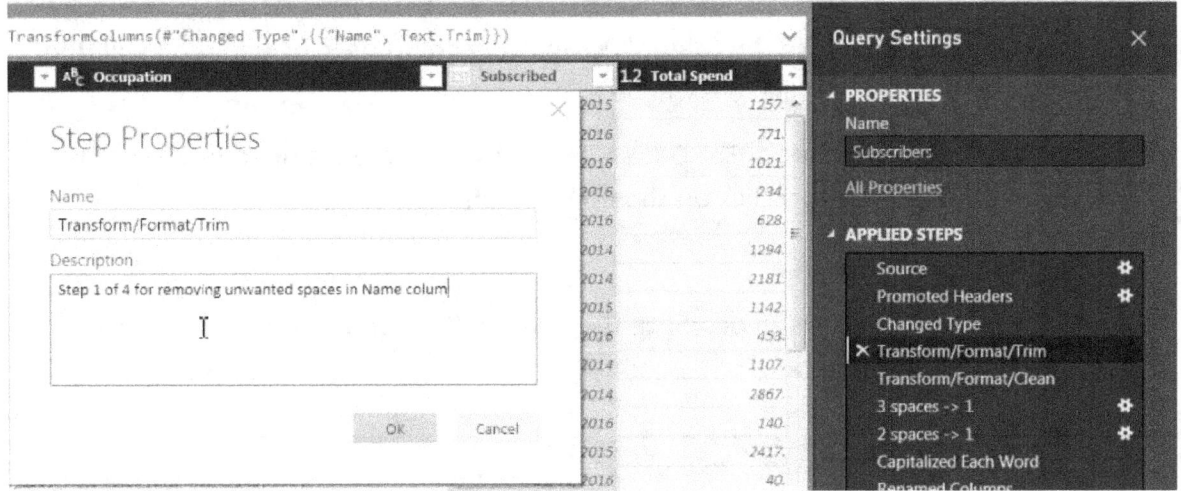

Then, of course, the next three steps would be steps 2, 3 and 4.

## Conclusion

When connecting to and transforming data, bear in mind that you have this useful ability to rename items and add metadata to the applied steps that are generated by Query Editor commands.

Using this facility helps to clarify the purpose of the operations which are being performed in the Query Editor.

## Chapter 4: The Split Columns Command

The Split Columns command in the Query Editor is very similar to Microsoft Excel's Text to Columns feature. It allows you to split a column using a delimiter or by a set number of characters.

In this example, we will use the folder "04-Splitting columns"; inside it you will find three text files, each of which we will be importing.

We start by choosing **Home > Get Data > Text/CSV**. The file we need is Clients.txt; to open it in the Query Editor, click on the **Edit** button.

### Tidying up the Data

The first thing we can do is to promote the header "Customer Code": **Transform > Use First Row as Headers.**

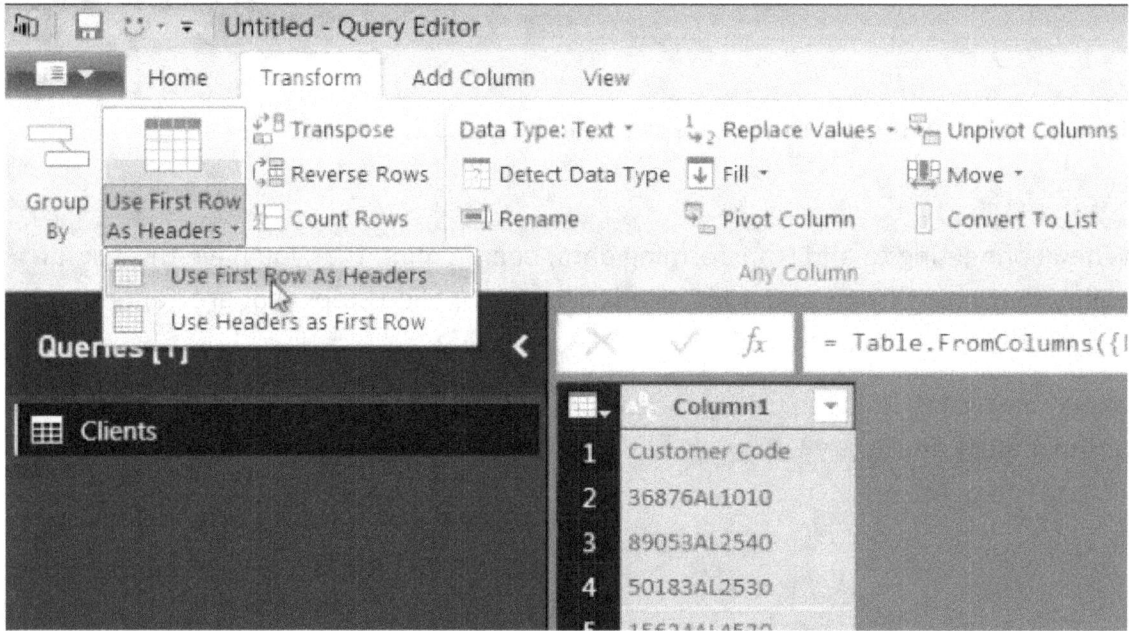

If we examine the Customer Code, we can see it consists of three parts: first we have a customer ID which consists of the first five characters; then we have a two-letter country code; and, finally, a four-character business sector code.

### Using Split by Number of Characters

To split the column, we can either **Right-click** on the column heading and chose to **Split**; or, in the Home Tab or the Ribbon, we will also find **Split Column > by Delimiter** and **Split Column > by Number of Characters**.

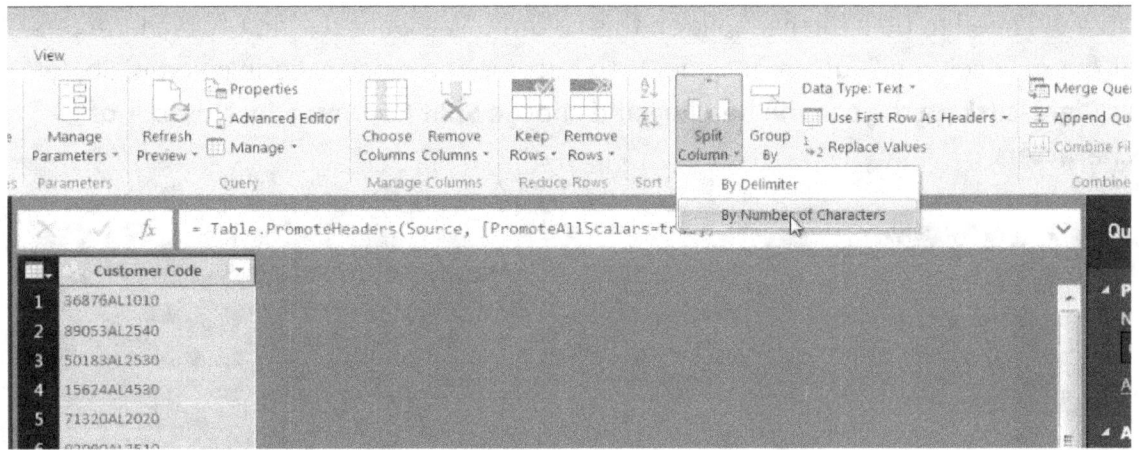

In this instance, we want to split by a set number of characters, once as far left as possible, and the number of characters we want is five.

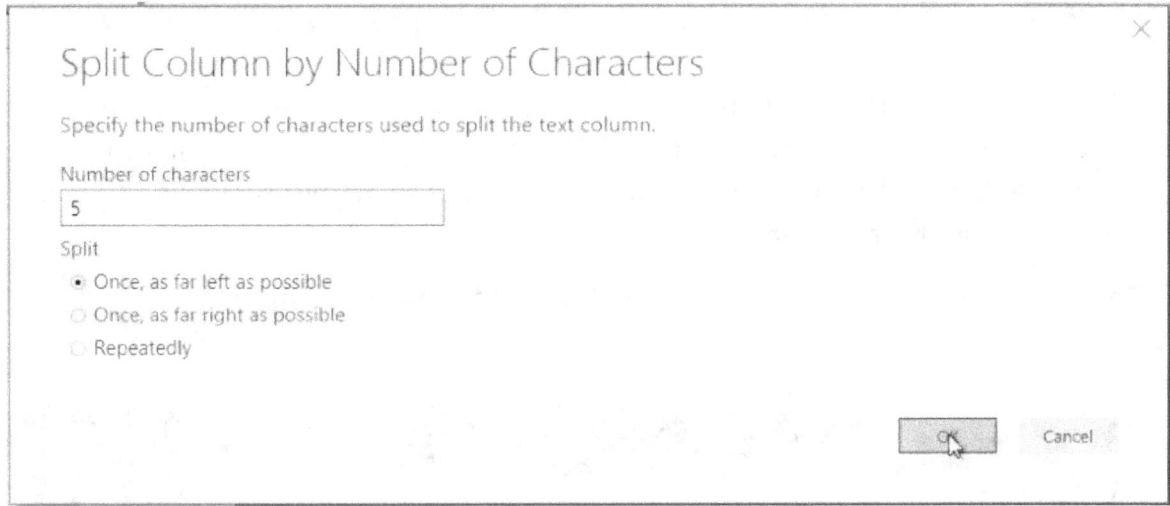

This command creates a step called "Split Column by Position"; but it also creates a second step called "Changed Type". Since the data is a customer ID, we do not actually need it to be changed. So, let us simply delete this automatically generated step by clicking on the X on the left of its name.

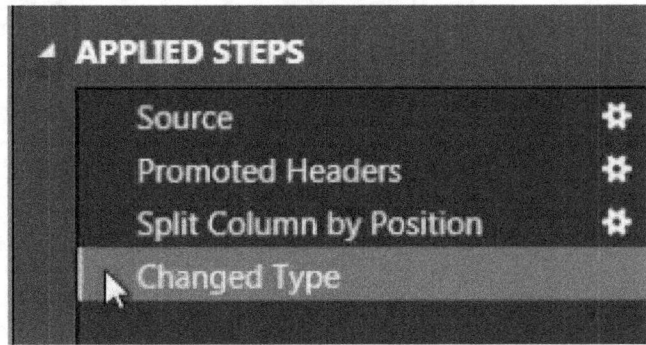

Now we need to do a further split on this column. We want the first two characters of the new column "Customer Code.2" to become the country code column. So, let us **Right-click** on the column heading and choose **Split Column > by Number of Characters**.

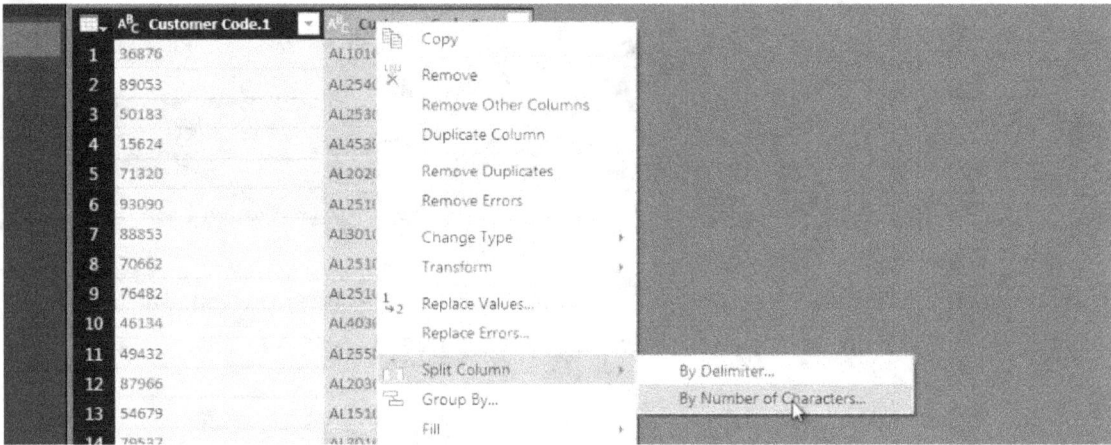

This time, again starting from the left, we want two characters. Again, the Query Editor has tried to be helpful, recognised numerical data and converted it into a whole number. In this example we would prefer it not to do this; so, let us get rid of this automatically generated step.

The final step is to rename the columns: "Customer Code", "Country Code" and "Sector Code".

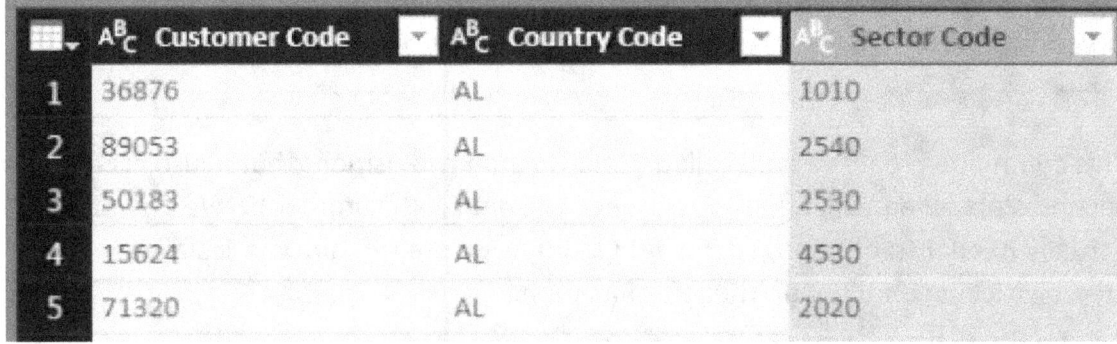

So, now that we have our clients' data sorted, we can import the two remaining text files: one containing country, and the other sector, information.

To import data while working in the Query Editor, we choose **Home > New Source > Text/CSV** and import the file "Countries.csv".

Because all the columns in this file are textual, the Promote Headers step has not been automatically generated for us. So, we need to use **Transform > Use first row as headers**.

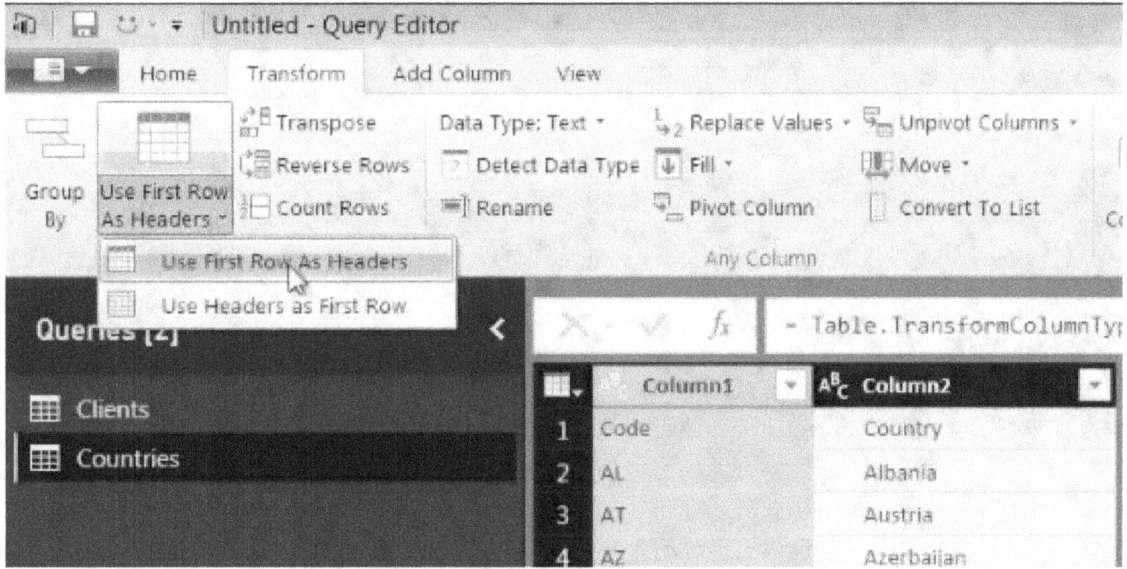

Finally, let us import the sector information: "Sectors.txt".

This time the promote headers is automatically generated for us; but we still have a Changed Type step which we do not want. We want to treat this as textual data, so let us get rid of the automatically generated step.

## Creating Relationships

So, our three tables are now good to go, and we can now create relationships between them so that we can display the spread of clients geographically and by business sector, so let us choose **Close & Apply**.

Next, we click on the Relationship button on the left of the screen, to link the tables together; because we did not rename the columns, so that the names of the common columns were identical, no relationships have been automatically generated.

We will therefore create the relationships manually; just drag from field to field. We drag from **Clients > Country Code** to **Countries > Code**; and from **Clients > Sector Code** to **Sectors > Code**.

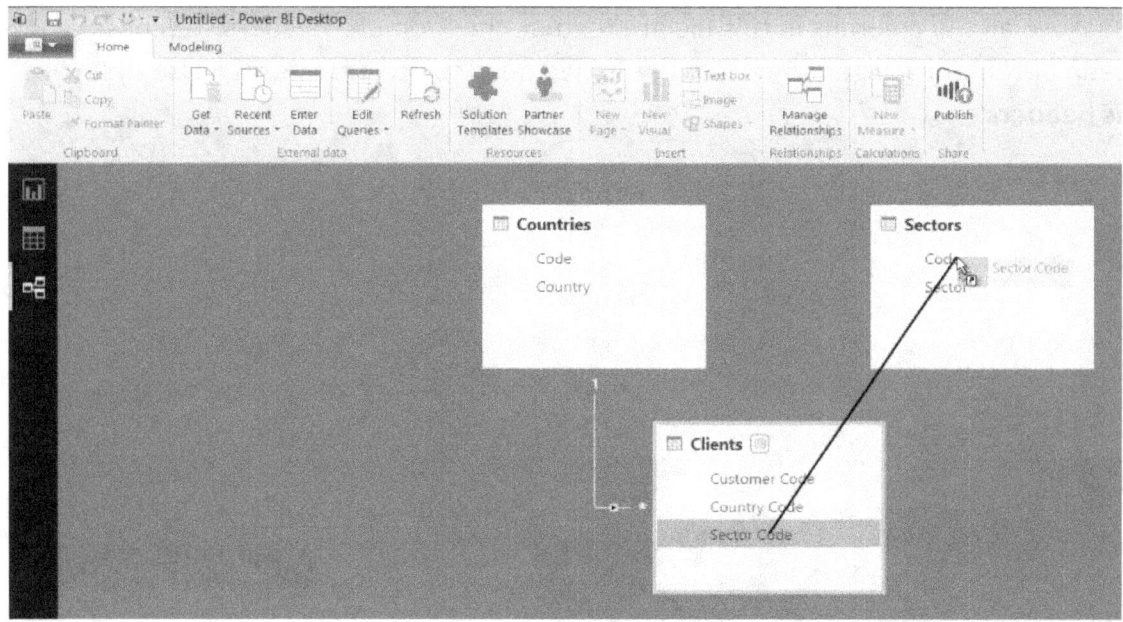

## Creating a Treemap Visual

With those relationships in place we can create a visual. We are going to use a treemap for this example.

First, let us rename the page "Sectors". Next, let us create a treemap visual and populate the visual with the name of the sector (Sectors > Sector). Then, from Clients, we can simply count the number of clients by adding Customer Code to the Values area. We can now see a nice breakdown of our customers in all the different business sectors.

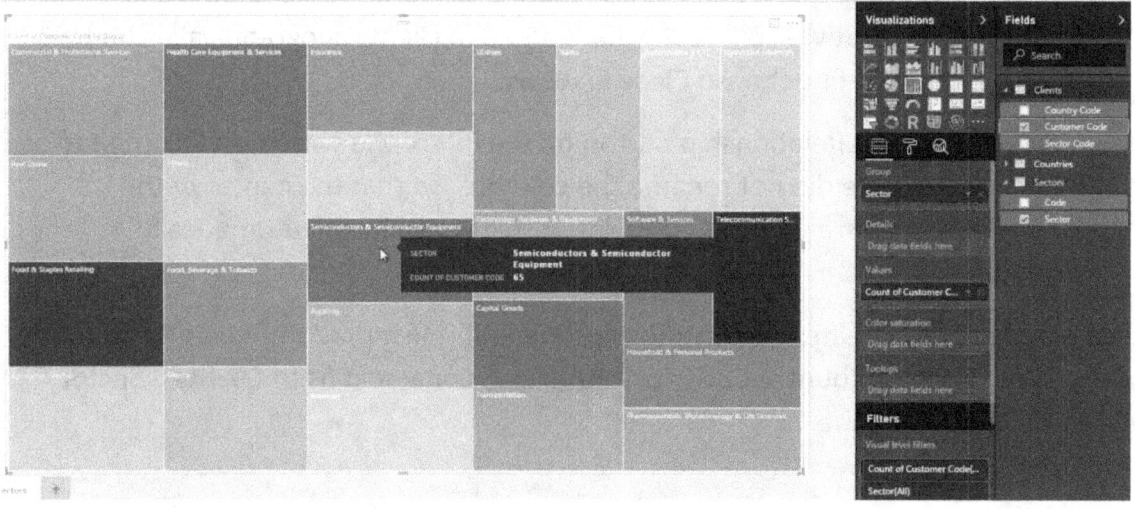

## Creating a Filled Map Visual

Finally, let us create a new page to show the world wide spread of our clients. This time we will use the Filled Map. This visual uses the saturation of the colour, super imposed on the map, to indicate the number of clients; the more intense the saturation of colour, the more clients in that area.

So, for Location, we use Country; for Colour Saturation we can use (Count of) Customer Code. We can now see that the intensity of the colour indicates the number of clients in that area. We have a lot of clients in the UK, hence the very intense colour, a few in the rest of Europe and then quite a lot in the United States.

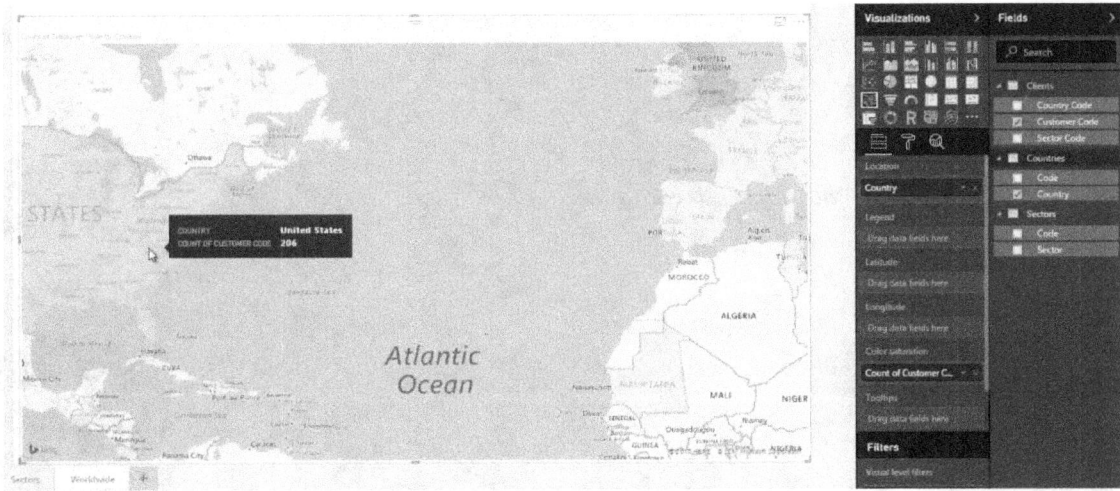

## Conclusion

In this chapter, you learned how to use the Split Column by Number of Characters command.

Using this command, we were able to create columns which could act as foreign keys, enabling us to create relationships with two other tables.

# Chapter 5: Removing Unwanted Rows

When you connect to data sources, it is quite often the case that your data does not start on row one. If the data has been automatically generated by another system, it may also contain some title information or some metadata preceding the data which you actually want. The Remove Rows command can be used to supress such data.

## Removing Header Rows

Let us examine an example. Using **Home > Get Data** in a blank Power BI Desktop file, load up the CSV file in the sub-folder "05-Removing rows". The file is called "Costs.csv".

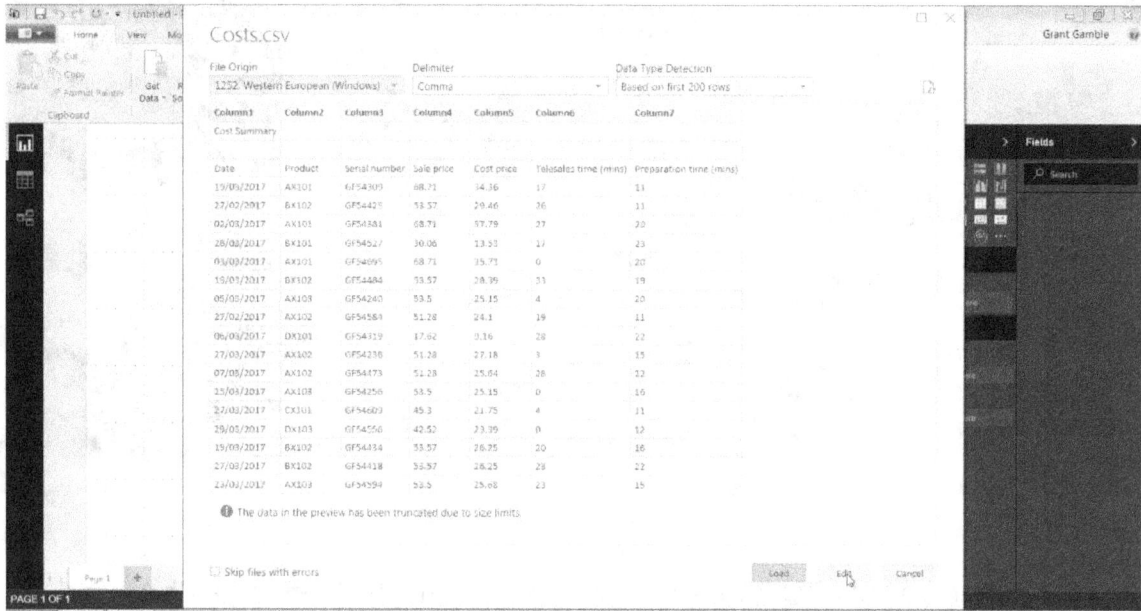

Click on **Edit** to enter the Query Editor; and, here, we will find that we simply have the title of the data on row 1 and then a blank row before the data starts. So, if we know that the report we are importing will always have this format, we can simply use the Remove Rows command to supress the first two rows.

You will find the command in the Home Tab of the Ribbon; we have **Keep Rows** and **Remove Rows.** If you have lots of rows to get rid of you can use Keep Rows, if there are only a few, you can use Remove Rows. In our example, we want to the remove top two rows.

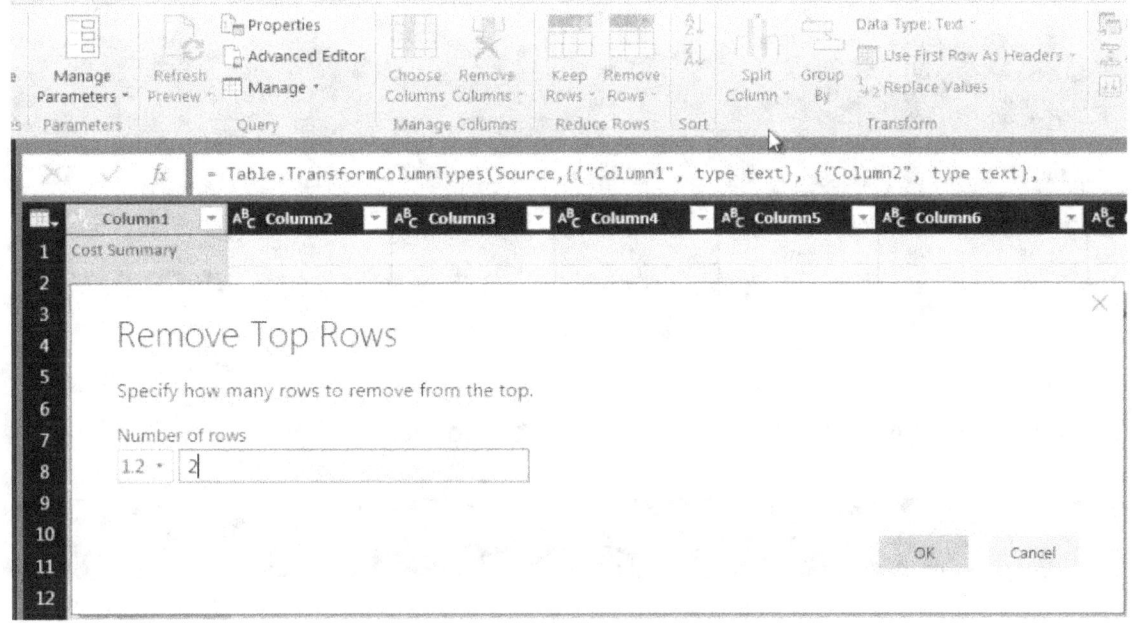

We are now left with our data and our headings, so the next logical step is to promote our headers; so, in the Home Tab of the Ribbon, we choose **Use First Row as Headers**.

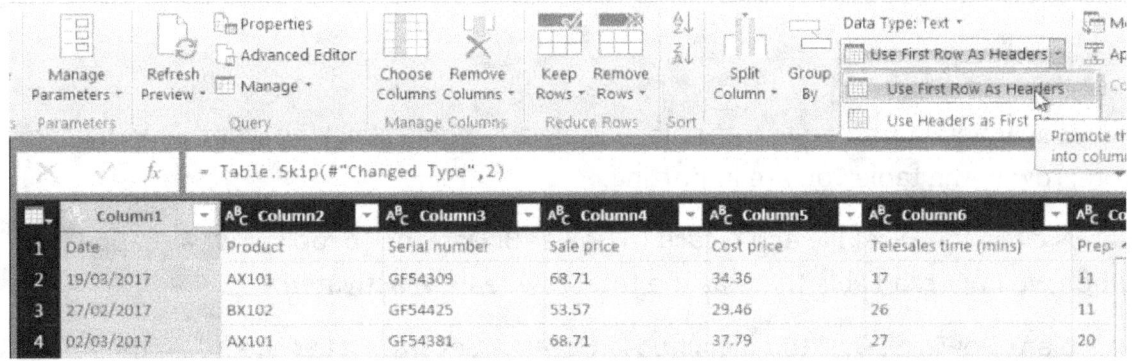

## Removing an Excel Table Total Row

Another common example of where it becomes necessary to remove rows is when you import an Excel table which uses the Total Row feature.

In the folder "05-Removing rows", open the file Costs.xlsx, in Excel. You will see that it contains an Excel table. If we move down to the bottom of the Table, you will notice there is a Total Row.

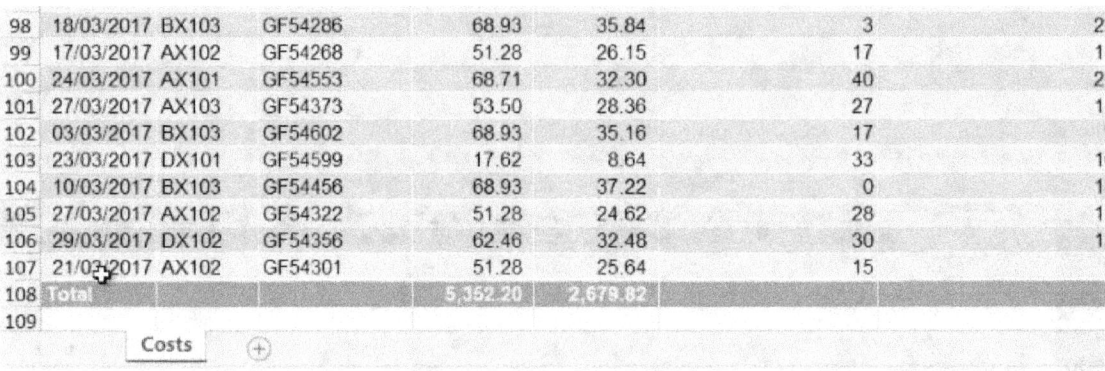

| | | | | | | | |
|---|---|---|---|---|---|---|---|
| 98 | 18/03/2017 | BX103 | GF54286 | 68.93 | 35.84 | 3 | 2 |
| 99 | 17/03/2017 | AX102 | GF54268 | 51.28 | 26.15 | 17 | 1 |
| 100 | 24/03/2017 | AX101 | GF54553 | 68.71 | 32.30 | 40 | 2 |
| 101 | 27/03/2017 | AX103 | GF54373 | 53.50 | 28.36 | 27 | 1 |
| 102 | 03/03/2017 | BX103 | GF54602 | 68.93 | 35.16 | 17 | |
| 103 | 23/03/2017 | DX101 | GF54599 | 17.62 | 8.64 | 33 | 1 |
| 104 | 10/03/2017 | BX103 | GF54456 | 68.93 | 37.22 | 0 | 1 |
| 105 | 27/03/2017 | AX102 | GF54322 | 51.28 | 24.62 | 28 | 1 |
| 106 | 29/03/2017 | DX102 | GF54356 | 62.46 | 32.48 | 30 | 1 |
| 107 | 21/03/2017 | AX102 | GF54301 | 51.28 | 25.64 | 15 | |
| 108 | Total | | | 5,362.20 | 2,679.82 | | |
| 109 | | | | | | | |

Costs

This feature is activated and deactivated in **Table Tools > Design**.

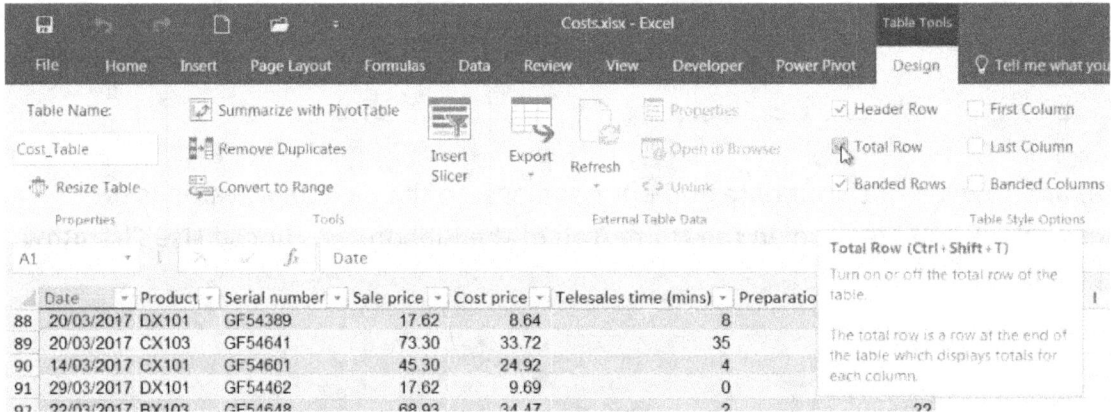

Whenever you import an Excel Table, it is always worth checking whether you have a total row in the table you are importing.

Let us close the Excel file and return to Power BI Desktop to look at what happens when we import a Table that has the total row feature activated.

In a blank Power BI Desktop file, choose **Home > Get Data > Excel;** and, in the folder "05-Removing rows", let us import the Excel file "Costs.xlsx". in the Preview window, select **Cost_Table** and then click on **Edit**.

If we know for a fact that the total row on this dataset is always activated, we could use the Remove Rows command. However, a more flexible approach is to use the second method which the Query Editor provides for removing unwanted rows of data; and that is to filter out the data which you want to remove.

If we check in the date column for the word "Total", then simply click in the check box to deactivate it, this will provide a better way of filtering out the data.

If we reload the data and there is no total row, we will not lose the last row of data, whereas, if we use the other approach, we run the risk of deleting a perfectly good data row. So, let us simply click in the checkbox next to "Total" to deactivate it and click **OK**.

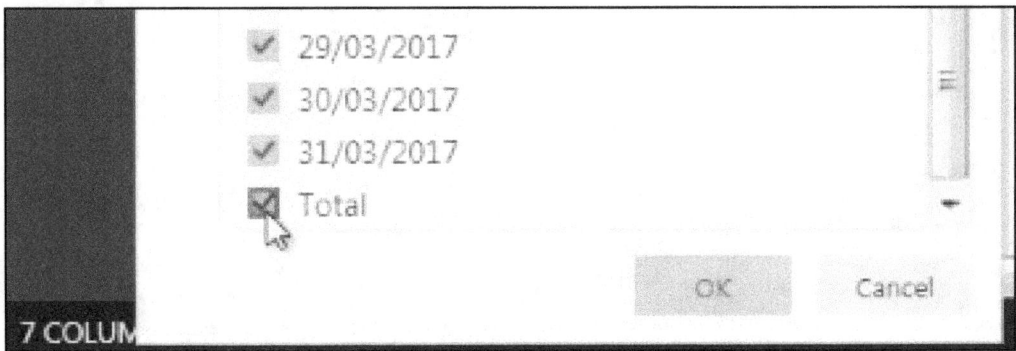

And, in a similar way, we could go to any of the number columns, and use number filters such as greater than, greater than or equal to, or between; all very useful. Perhaps the most useful of all are the date filters.

Date filters provide several options which are volatile, in that they are based on the current date. For example, you can choose **Week > Last Week** to display all dates which fall within a week of the current date.

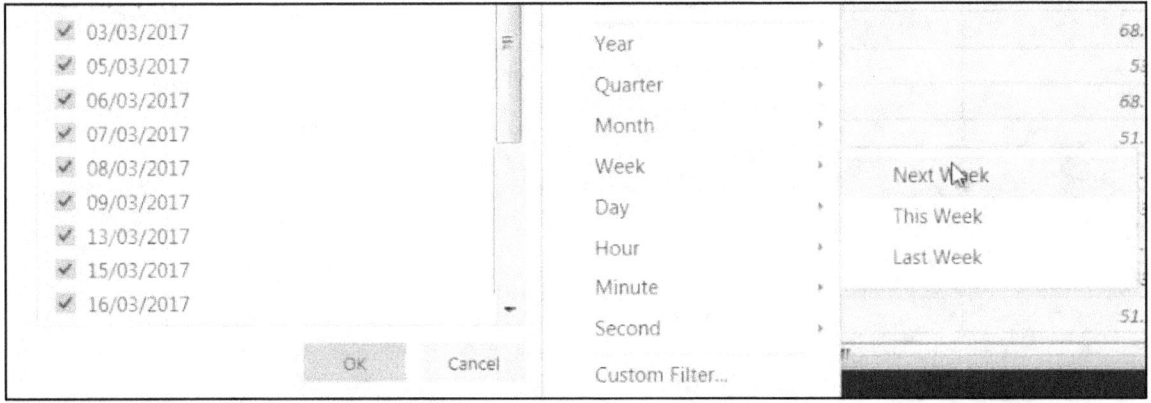

## Conclusion

These, then, are the two key methods of removing data which you do not want to import.

You can do so by either removing X number of rows from top or bottom or by filtering out any data that is irrelevant for your purposes.

# Chapter 6: Replace Value and Fill Down

In this chapter, we will look at the Replace Value and Fill Down commands. Both are very useful where you want to make modifications to the data, the actual content that you are importing.

To illustrate their use, let us import the data with which we will be working. Click **Home > Get Data > Text/CSV** and import the only text file inside the "06 Replace Values" folder, "London expenses 2016". To open the data in the Query Editor, click on **Edit**.

Before we can start working with the data, we have two steps to perform. Firstly, we have two unwanted rows to remove. As we saw previously, we do this by using **Remove Rows** command; **Remove Top Rows** in this case, removing two rows. Next, we create a Promote Headers step, by choosing to **Use First Row as Headers**.

## The Replace Values Command

Now let us turn our attention to the Replace Values command. We will begin with the currency symbol in the amount column, we have the pound currency symbol followed by a space, in addition to this we also have some rows which contain the text "not agreed". Let us deal with the £ first. Even if you do not remove currency symbols, simply by changing the data type, for currency you normally use fixed decimal number will usually successfully convert the value to a number and remove the currency symbol.

If you want to tread more carefully you can manually remove the currency symbol yourself, just so that you are explicitly saying: "I do not want any currency symbols there when I attempt the conversion".

As with most Power Query commands, we can find Replace Values by **Right-click**ing on the column heading. Additionally, it is available in the Home Tab. The value we are looking for is the Pound sign followed by a space; and we are replacing it with nothing.

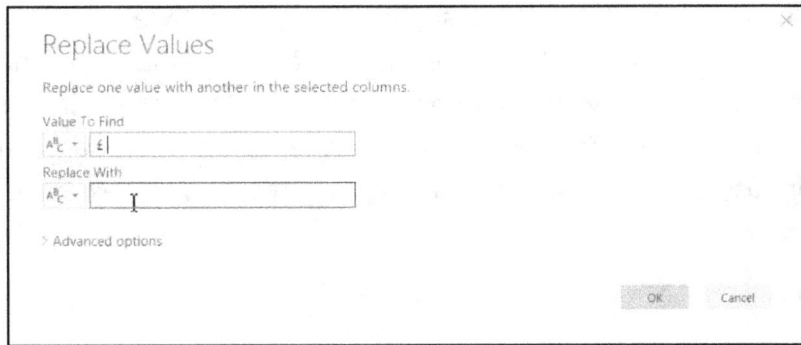

Next, we can think about the text values. A good way of isolating these is to click on the filter drop down and look for text values that shouldn't be there. If you simply want to remove them, you can then just switch them off.

The problem with his approach, of course, is that it assumes the same values will always be present. Let us say in our case our users are in the habit of typing in a comment whenever an amount is not available, so the term "not agreed" could be replaced by any number of equivalent comments entered by different users.

## Remove Errors and Replace Errors

The logical way of proceeding would be, therefore, to convert the data type of the Amount column to currency (fixed decimal number), knowing that any text values will generate an error.

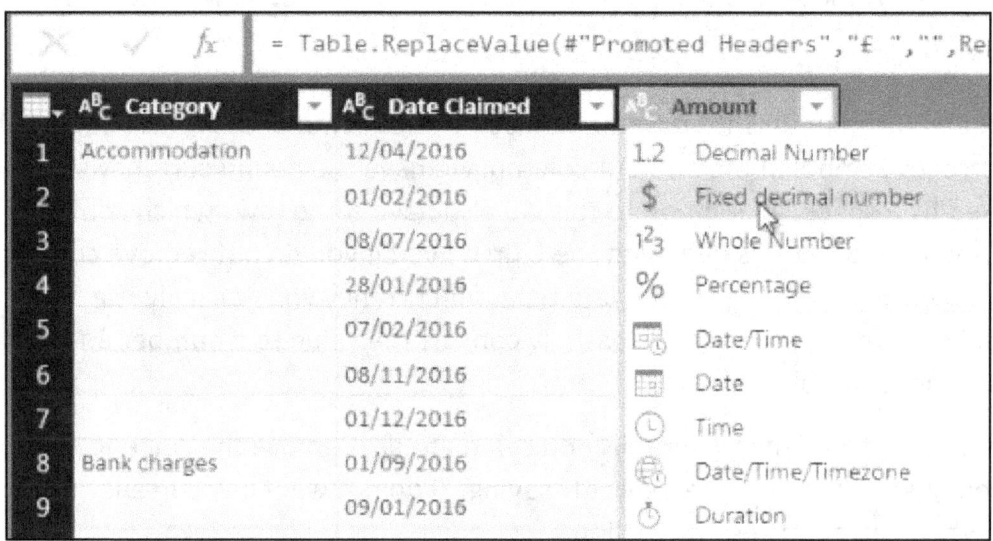

We can then use the Remove Errors step to remove these rows. Or, better still, we can use Replace Errors, leaving the rows in place and entering the most suitable numeric value in the Amount column.

You will find the Replace Errors command on **Right-click > Transform**. This command gives us a bit more flexibility; we could say for example that we would like a zero to appear in place of the error; that way the transaction will remain present in the dataset, but it will simply have an amount of zero. We may also decide that, from experience, most of these expense claims are settled and that, for analysis purposes, it may be more useful to enter an arbitrary figure; let us say, for example, £50.

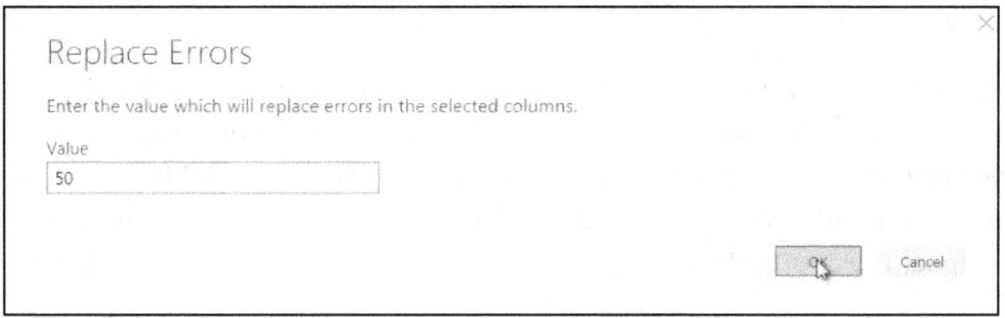

Let us also perform one final Replace Values operation. Click the filter drop down on the right of the Category column heading.

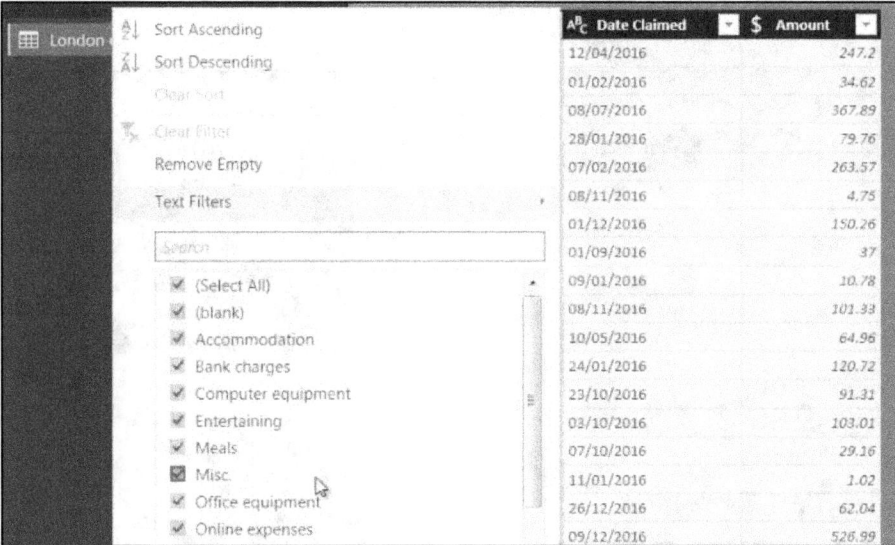

Let us say we do not like the fact that the word miscellaneous is abbreviated, unlike all the other terms. Let us, therefore, perform, a straightforward **Replace Values** step, using "Misc." as the **Value to find,** and "Miscellaneous" as the **Replace with** value.

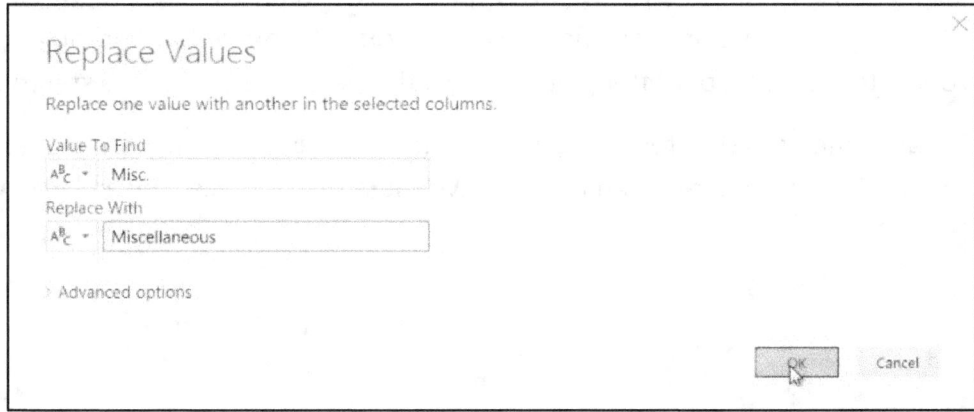

## The Fill Down Command

Moving onto Fill Down; this is a command designed to correct a problem encountered when connecting to data which is, in reality, a report generated by another system. It is not uncommon for this type of data to use subheadings within a column, which means that we have a lot of rows which are blank, but which should really repeat the appropriate subhead.

Fill Down is more commonly used than Fill Up; but once you have used Fill Down, you can see exactly how Fill Up would work. If we are going to analyze the dataset to which we have connected, we must have a value on every row of the Category column. Instead, we simply have, for example, "Accommodation" acting as a heading, rather than as a data entry.

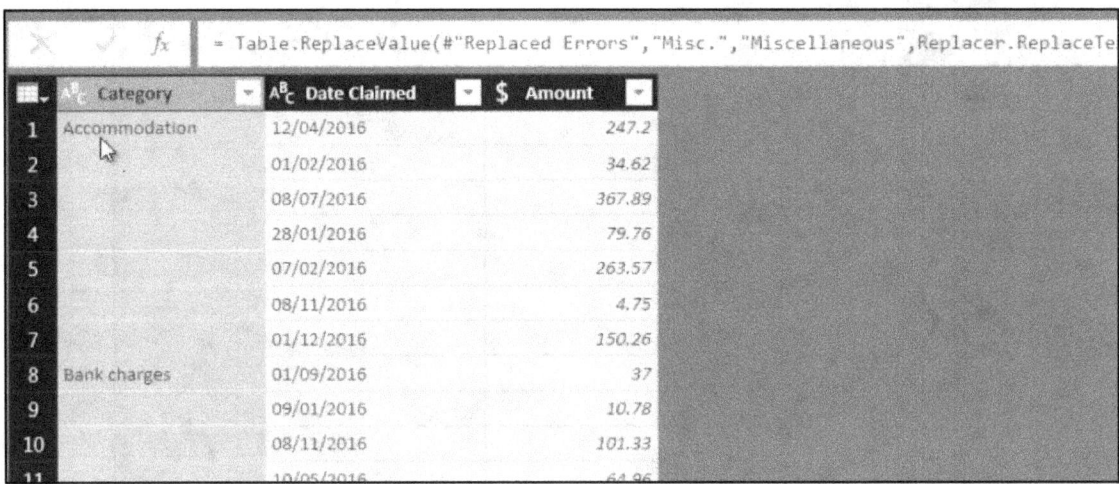

The Fill Down command will take each of these headings and copy it down into the blank rows below; but it will never overwrite an entry, since only empty rows will ever be filled.

However, the Fill commands will only replace null values, and Power BI does not treat a blank entry as null. Thus, if we attempt to fill the blank rows by **Right-click**ing on the Category column and choosing **Fill Down**, you will notice that, although the **Filled Down** step is created; nothing happens to the data; the blanks are still there.

This is because the cells that follow each entry are not null cells; they are blank. Before the Fill Down command can be used, we must first replace these blanks with nulls.

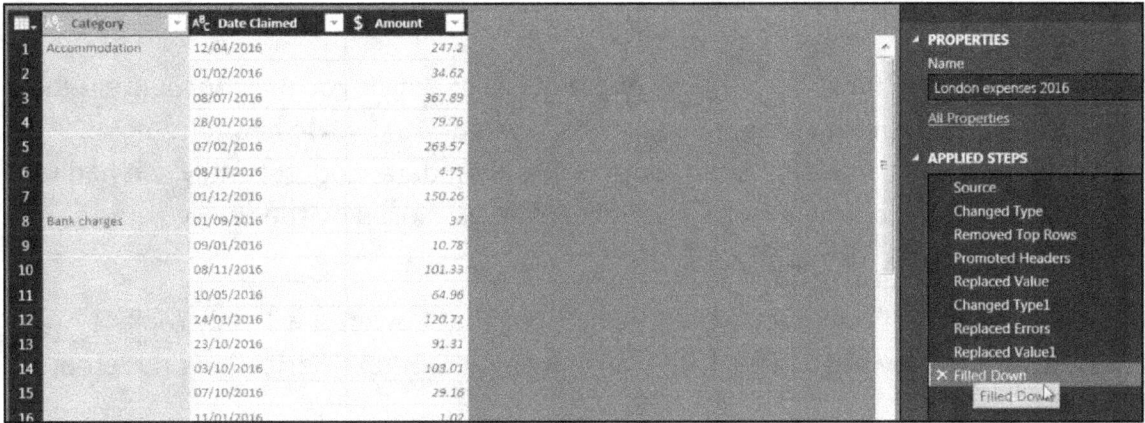

Let us delete the **Filled Down** step and then use Replace Values to insert nulls instead of blanks; entering nothing in **Value to find,** and "null" in **Replace with**.

Now that we have null values, if we use Fill Down again, it will produce the desired result.

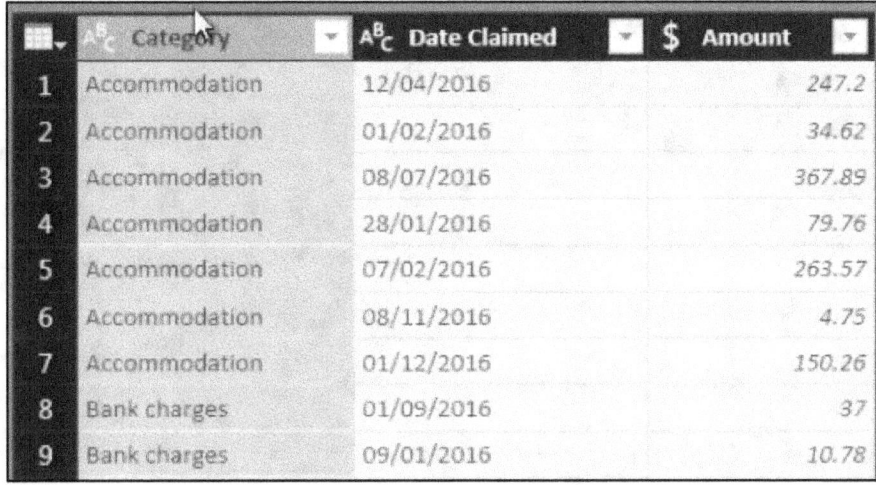

To finish, let us change the data type of the date claimed column to date.

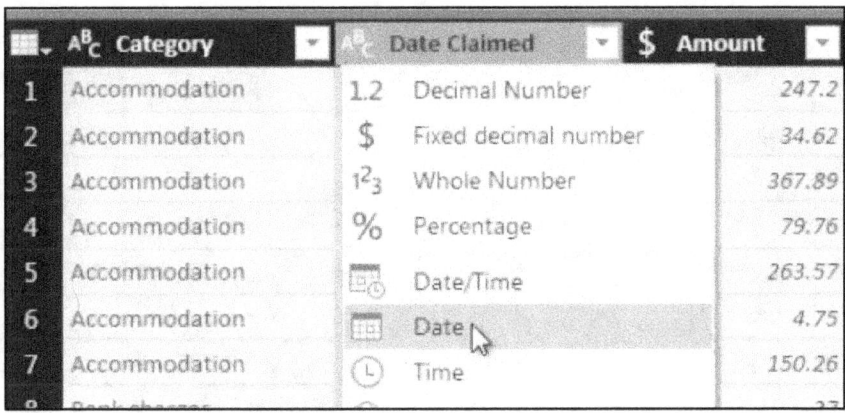

38

## Conclusion

In this chapter, we have looked at a couple of issues which you may encounter when connecting to a report generated by another system. Firstly, we had to remove leading rows which contained metadata rather than data; and, secondly, we had to use the Fill Down command to replace blank values caused by the use of sub-headings within the data body.

When using the Fill Down command, remember that Power BI will only replace null values; so, you may need to replace blanks with nulls before performing this step.

The Replace Values command is useful where the value(s) to be replaced are known in advance.

When replacing unknown values, it is sometimes possible to deliberately perform an operation which converts all these values into errors; and then to use the Remove Errors or Replace Errors command.

# Chapter 7: The Unpivot Columns Command

## What is Pivoted Data?

As we have seen, Power BI allows you to connect to lots of different data sources; and it is inevitable that, from time to time, the data source to which you are connecting is going to be a report generated by another system.

One of the attributes that reports sometimes contain is pivoting, which is where the members of a category have been separated out into columns. The following illustration shows an example using Excel data.

Here is the source data.

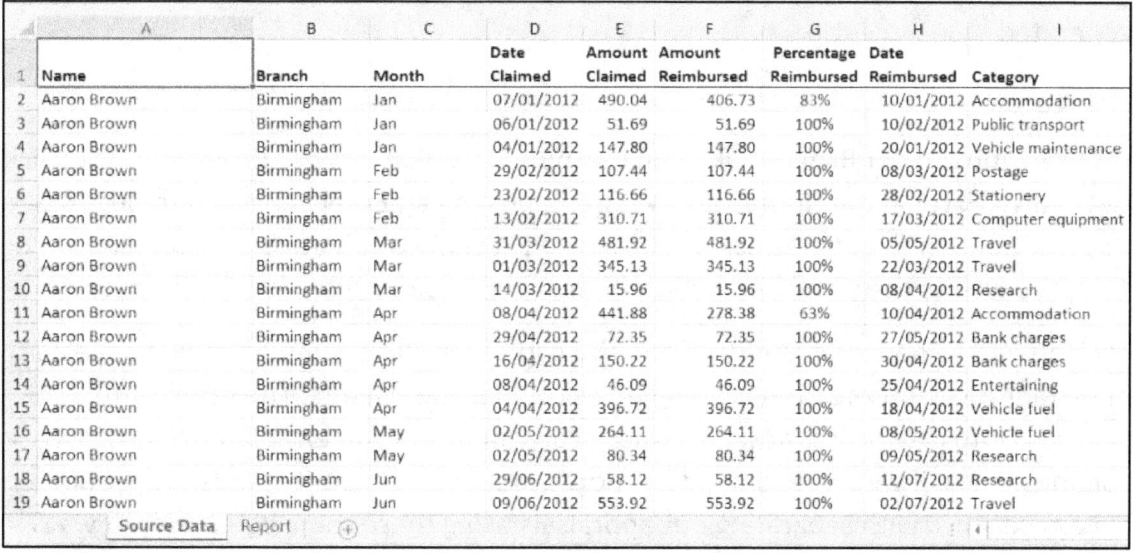

And, here is a pivot Table based on that source data.

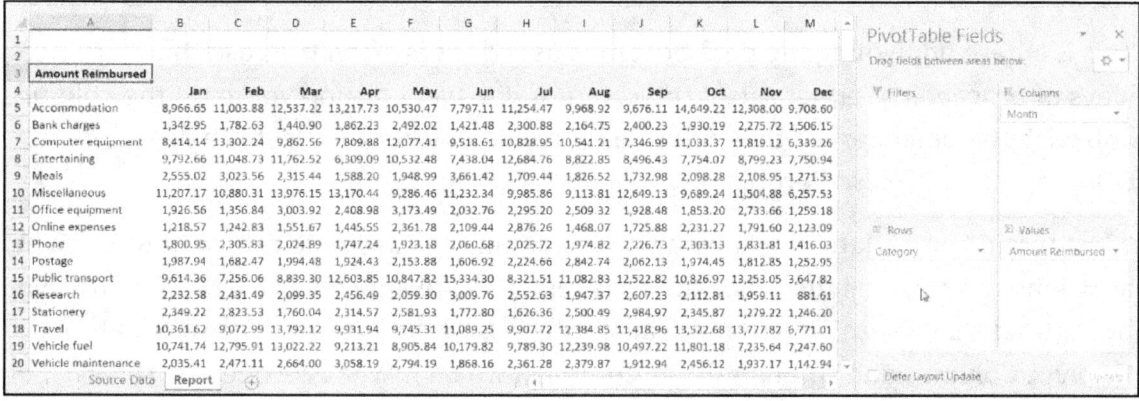

As you can see we have Category arranged in rows; we have Month arranged in columns and the value which we are analysing is Amount Reimbursed.

40

Ideally, we would want to import the raw data into Power BI, since this will give us the maximum amount of flexibility. In the case of Excel, pivoting is often easy to avoid, or to reverse; and I should also point out that you cannot import data directly from an Excel pivot table into Power BI. However, many systems also output reports in this same pivoted format; and it is here that you will encounter situations where unpivoting is required.

The problematic aspect, in the above illustration, is the fact that months are separated out into columns, or, pivoted. Whenever you connect to a report with this feature, Power BI's Unpivot command will reverse the pivoting and reduce the separate columns down to two columns: one, containing a description; and, the other, a value. The entries which were headings in the report will become entries within the description column and as many extra rows as necessary will be generated.

## Importing the Data

Let us go into Power BI and look at an example. In a blank Power BI Desktop file, click **Get Data > Excel** in the Home Tab. We are importing an Excel file; so, in folder "07-Unpivot Columns", double-click on the single Excel file Unpivot.xlsx. It contains a Table; as well as the worksheet which houses the Table, which we can ignore.

Click on **Edit** to open the Query Editor. We can see in this example that we have a list of restaurants with the ratings assigned to them by our clients. The ratings are arranged into categories; however, these categories have been split into separate columns. Thus, if we were to build a report using this data, as it stands, we would always be stuck with separating out appraisals using these same categories. If we were interested in doing a comparison of the popularities of the different restaurants, then we would be stuck.

## Using UnPivot Other Columns

This is where unpivoting the data becomes useful. As is often the case there are two ways of proceeding; either select the columns you want to unpivot, or, if the columns you wish to unpivot are in the minority, it may be quicker to select the other columns; as is the case here.

"Restaurant" and "Date" are the only two columns which we do not want to unpivot; as we move across, all the other columns relate to the appraisal. We can find unpivot by **Right-click**ing or going into the Transform Tab, where we have the two features **Unpivot Columns** and **Unpivot other Columns**, which is what we need on this occasion.

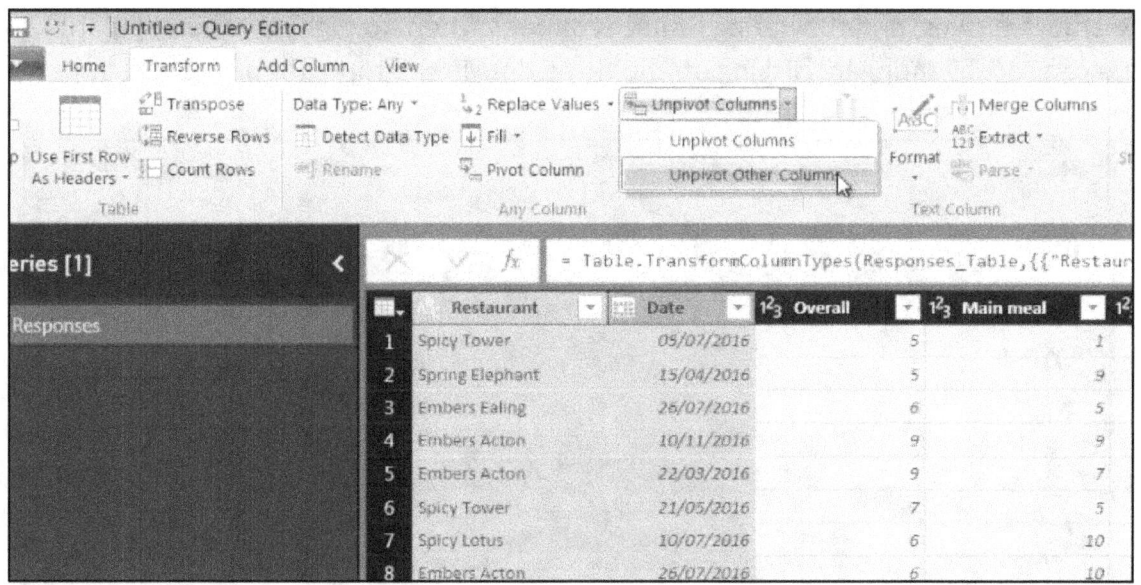

When you unpivot columns, you end up with two columns, named "Attributes" and "Values". The "Attribute" column contains the original column headings, while the "Values" column contains the entries which were underneath each of those headings. The Query Editor automatically marries everything up for you, creating as many extra rows as necessary.

Our final step is simply to rename these two resulting columns; so, let us replace "Attribute" with "Category" and "Values" with "Rating".

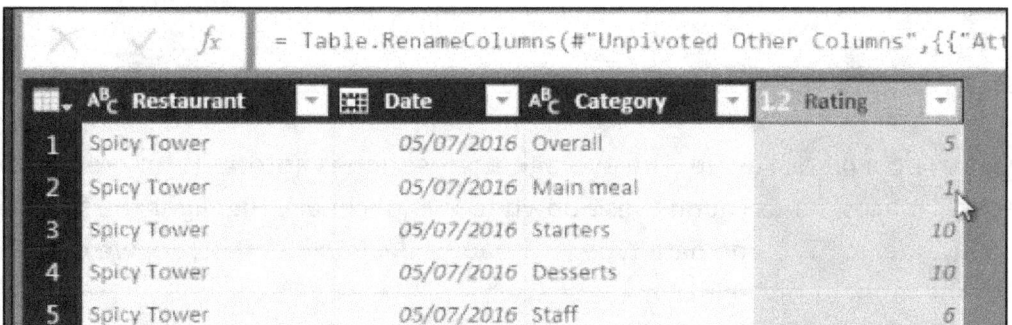

We now have a much more flexible dataset for building reports. Let us perform one final check by ensuring that the Change Type step has done a good job. We can see we have a decimal number for the rating and a date for the date. This looks fine, so we are good to click **Close & Apply**.

## Creating a Bar Chart Visual

Let us now create a visual to highlight the popularity of our individual restaurants. Bar charts are good for these comparisons; and we simply need to activate the

Restaurant (Axis) and the Rating (Value) columns. Then, to highlight the popularity, we can sort by rating by clicking on the three dots in the top right of the visual.

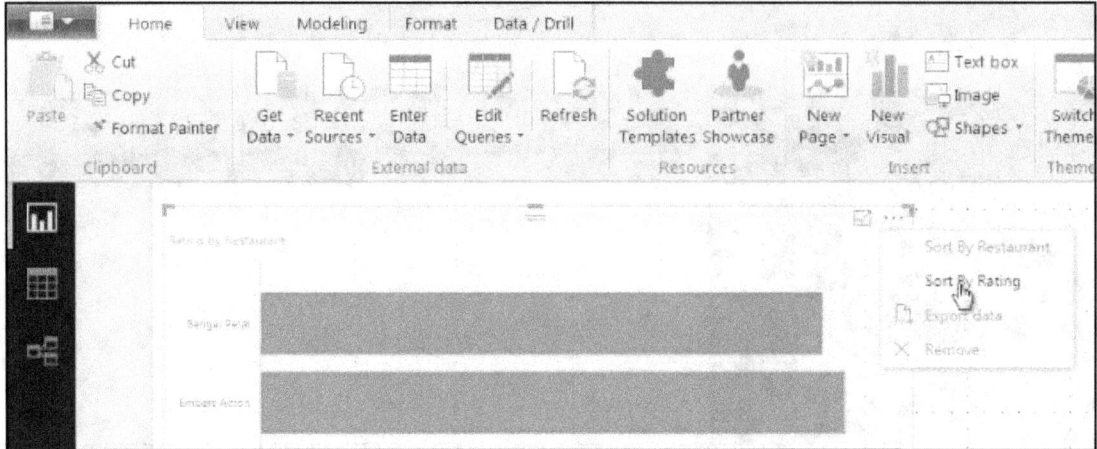

The default aggregation for any numeric field is always Sum; however, here, we will need to change it to Average by clicking on the arrow to the right of Rating.

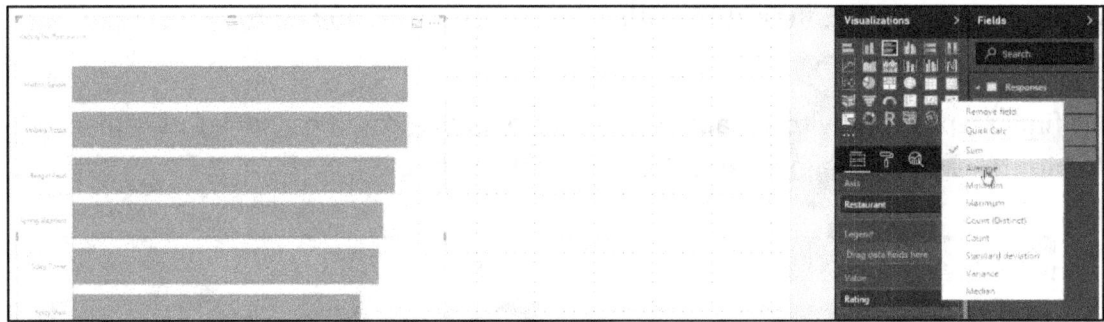

Now let us do a bit of tidy up. The average aggregation is notorious for creating lots of decimal places; let us round these down to two decimals. Highlight the field rating, then, in Modelling Tab, the data type is already a decimal number; so, we can simply change the number of decimal places to two.

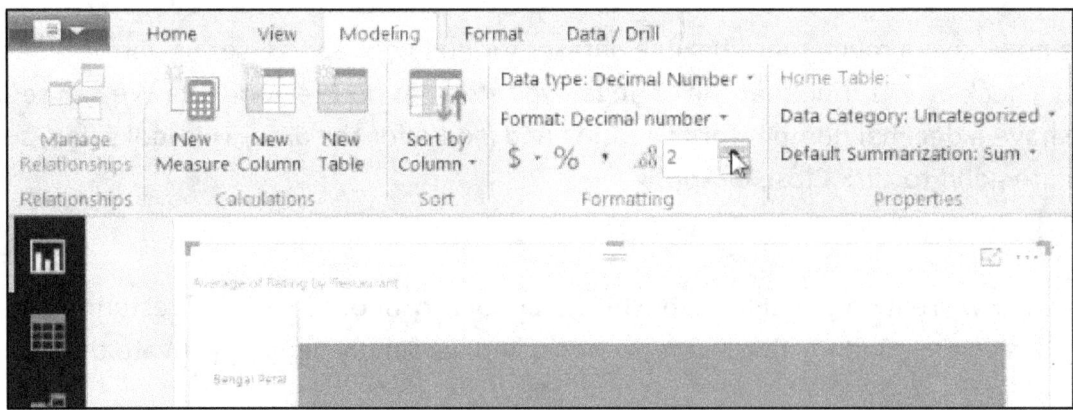

Next, let us increase the text size on the two axes and on the title.

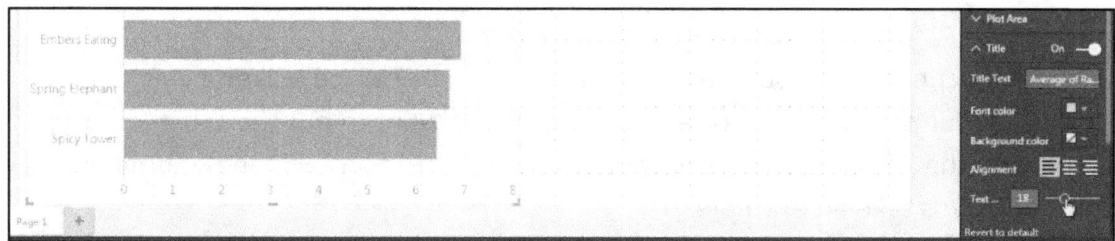

We can also change the title to "Restaurant Popularity".

By unpivoting the data, we have now been able to focus on analysing restaurant popularity, but we can still use the categories we had pivoted as a secondary item. We can do that by creating a category slicer.

To do this make sure you deselect any selected items; otherwise you will end up converting that item into the type of visual on which you click. Click on the slicer visual and activate the Category field.

To increase the size of the text in the slicer, look in **Format > Items**.

Now we can see which restaurants are the most popular in each of the different categories. Thus, for example, we can see that Bengal Petal is the overall most popular and it keeps popping up in a lot of different categories; but it is especially strong in the Overall category; and so forth.

## Conclusion

Pivoting refers to the situation where a report which you are importing into Power BI has separated, or pivoted, the members of a field into their own separate column headings.

Unpivoting report data gives you a lot more flexibility as to how you can analyze this data in your reports.

The Unpivot Other Columns is useful in that it allows you to unpivot columns without having to know the name of the columns or their number.

## Chapter 8: Reordering Columns

### Benefits of Changing Column Order

When connecting to data sources, reordering columns can be a useful way of improving your productivity. For example, you may want to put the most important columns on the left; or, you may want to group related or important columns together. Let us take an example.

We will begin by bringing in some Excel data; so, work your way into the folder "08-Reordering Columns"; and, here, you will find the Excel file "All Patient Data.xlsx".

This file contains a single Excel worksheet, not a Table; and one possible consequence of bringing in data from an Excel worksheet, rather than from a table, is that you often find extra blank columns are imported as part of the dataset. So, in addition to reordering columns we will also need to remove some columns.

Click **Edit** to go into the Query Editor. As always, a few automated steps have been created for us, the change type is a little premature as we will be doing quite a few modifications, so we can delete this step.

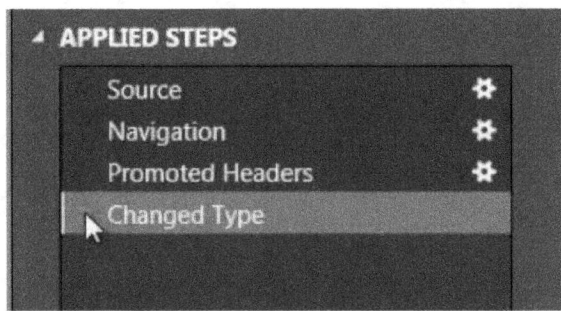

Let me also remind you that, if you want to stop the editor from automatically inserting these Changed Type steps, you can go into **File > Options > Options and Settings**; then, in the **CURRENT FILE** section, click **Data Load** and switch off the option **Automatically detect column types and headers for unstructured sources**.

Let us begin with column removal. Scroll across to the right to the extra, unwanted columns which have been imported. Click and Shift-click on the first and last column headers, respectively; then, you can either **Right-click**, or, in the **Home** Tab, choose **Remove Columns**.

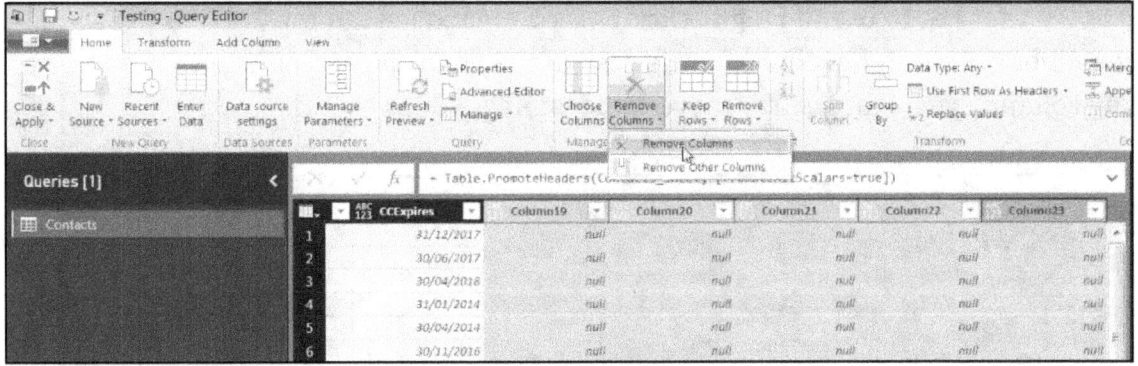

## Moving Columns by Dragging

There are two main techniques for reordering columns, the first is to move one or more selected columns to a specific position, this is done simply by dragging left or right. Thus, if we want to move the Blood Type column after the Weight and Height columns, we simply select that column, click on the heading and drag left or right.

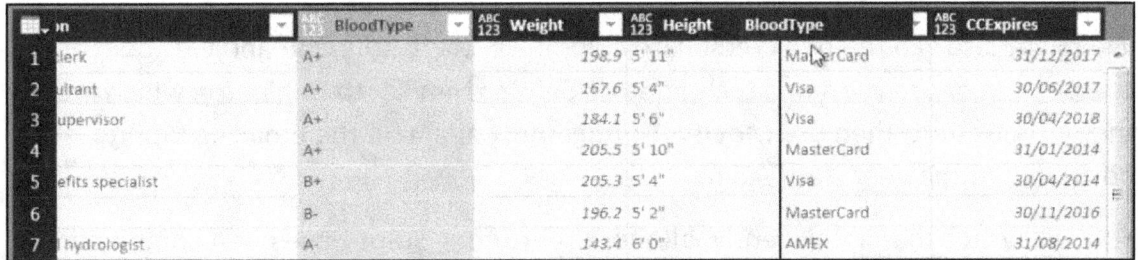

A bold vertical bar will indicate the new position of the column as you drag. When this bar is in the correct position, you simply release to insert the column.

## Moving Columns Relative to Other Columns

The second technique is to move one or more columns relative to the other columns. For example, if we want to treat Email as the key column and, therefore, to be the first column, we can simply highlight the column; and then, either **Right-click** and select Move, and choose one of the options for moving the column. We can either move it one place to the left, one place to the right, to the very beginning, or to the very end.

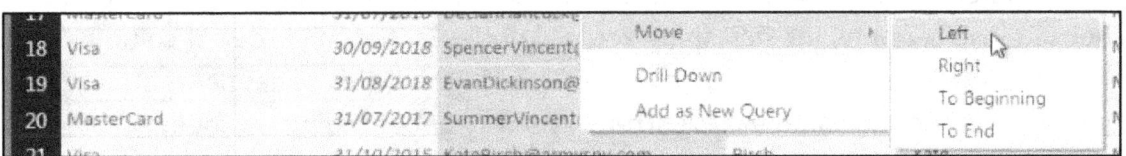

If you prefer not to use the **Right-click**, this command lives in the Transform Tab of the Ribbon. Thus, for example, in the case of the email address, if we want it to be a key column, we might just say move to beginning.

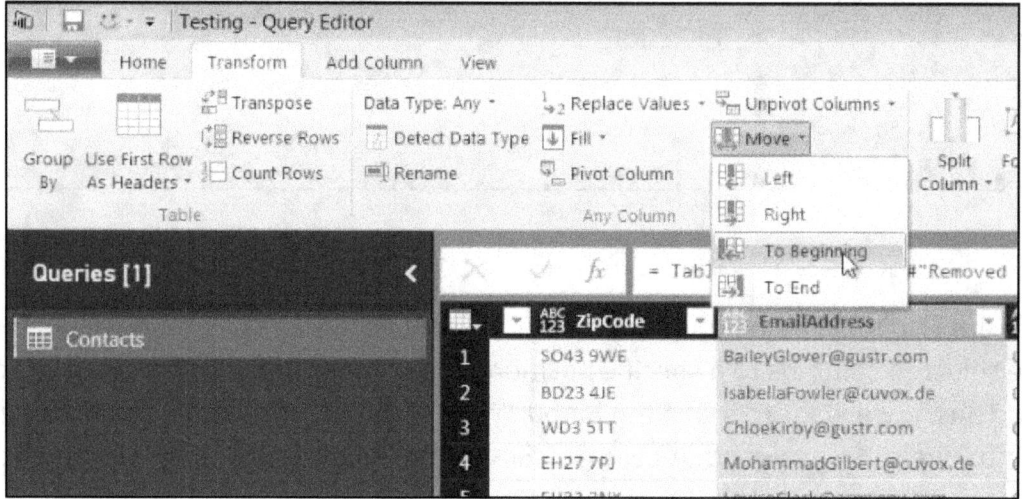

We might also like the two credit card columns at the beginning; and we could of course drag or use the same technique as before: **Move > to Beginning** which moves them to the start; then use **Move > To Beginning** again on the email column to position it at the very start again.

You will notice that, intelligently, all these reordering steps have been combined into a single Reorder Columns step.

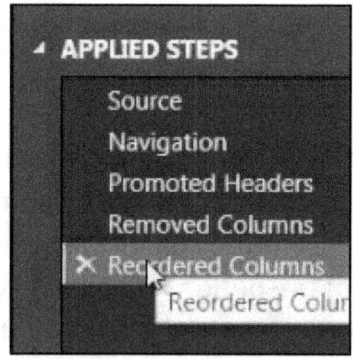

The Query Editor is the only place in which you can reorder columns; so, once you choose **Close & Apply**, the first thing you will notice is that the order of columns has no impact on the order in which fields are listed in the Fields pane; fields are always listed alphabetically, and there is currently no way of overriding this behaviour.

However, when you switch to Data view, the order of columns that you specified in the Query Editor is preserved; though you will notice that you have no way of modifying the order any further; it is only in the Query Editor that you can change the order.

Going back into the Query Editor, we will continue working with this same example in the next chapter when we look at creating custom columns.

## Conclusion

Reordering columns is useful when you work with tables containing a lot of columns.

Columns may be moved by dragging or by choosing an option in the **Move** drop-down menu.

If all the move operations are performed together, they will generate only one step in the Applied Steps pane.

## Chapter 9: Creating Custom Columns

In this chapter, we will carry on from where we left off in the last chapter and move on to look at the creation of custom columns. Just to remind you that, when working with tables that have a lot of columns, you can always close the navigation pane by clicking on its minimise button.

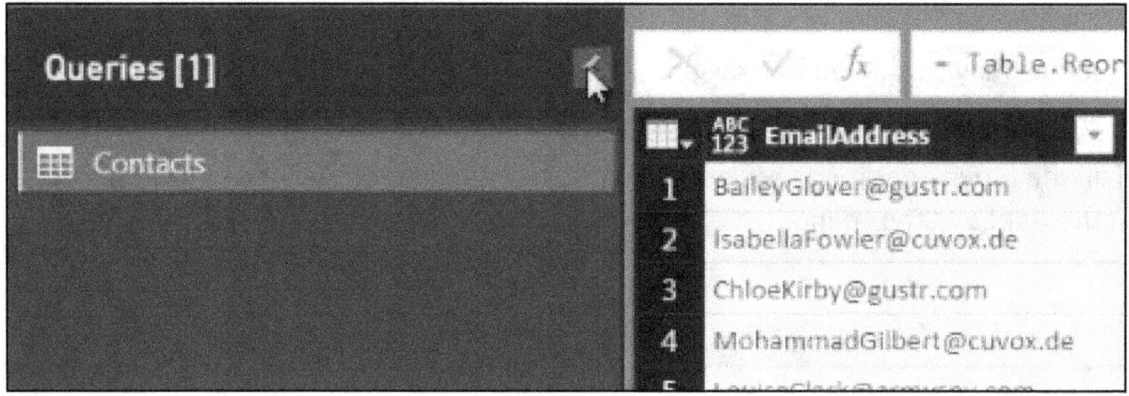

You can also close the Query Settings, but one does tend to need to leave it open to keep an eye on the steps which one is creating, or which are being automatically generated.

We can close it and, if we need it open again, we can go to **View > Query Settings**. The two columns we will be creating will be a Height in Inches column and a Body Mass Index (or BMI) column. The (imperial) BMI can be calculated from the weight in pounds and the height in inches. You can, therefore, see why we need a new Height column; currently, Height is a text column containing both feet and inches; e.g., 5' 11".

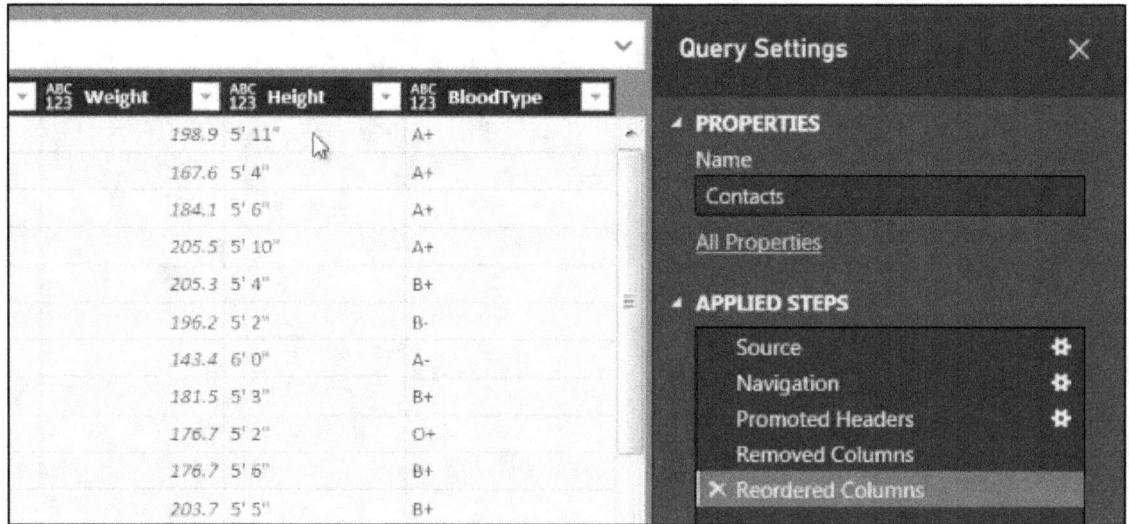

So, for analysis purposes we could not use this column. We will create a new Height column, containing just inches, which can then be converted to a numeric data type.

## Using Split by Delimiter

As this is an intro course, we are going to do it in the simplest manner possible by using a series of steps, the M language can allow you to create a column and just enter a formula and we will discuss techniques like this in the advanced course. The first step we will use is to split the Height column, using apostrophe as the delimiter. To do this, we highlight the column, **Right-click** and choose **Split Column > by Delimiter** and specify the delimiter which will be Custom, then apostrophe. In the following illustration, we are using **Split at left most delimiter**; however, this should have no impact on the result, as there will only be one occurrence in each entry.

In **Advanced** options you will also notice an option to specify the quote character.

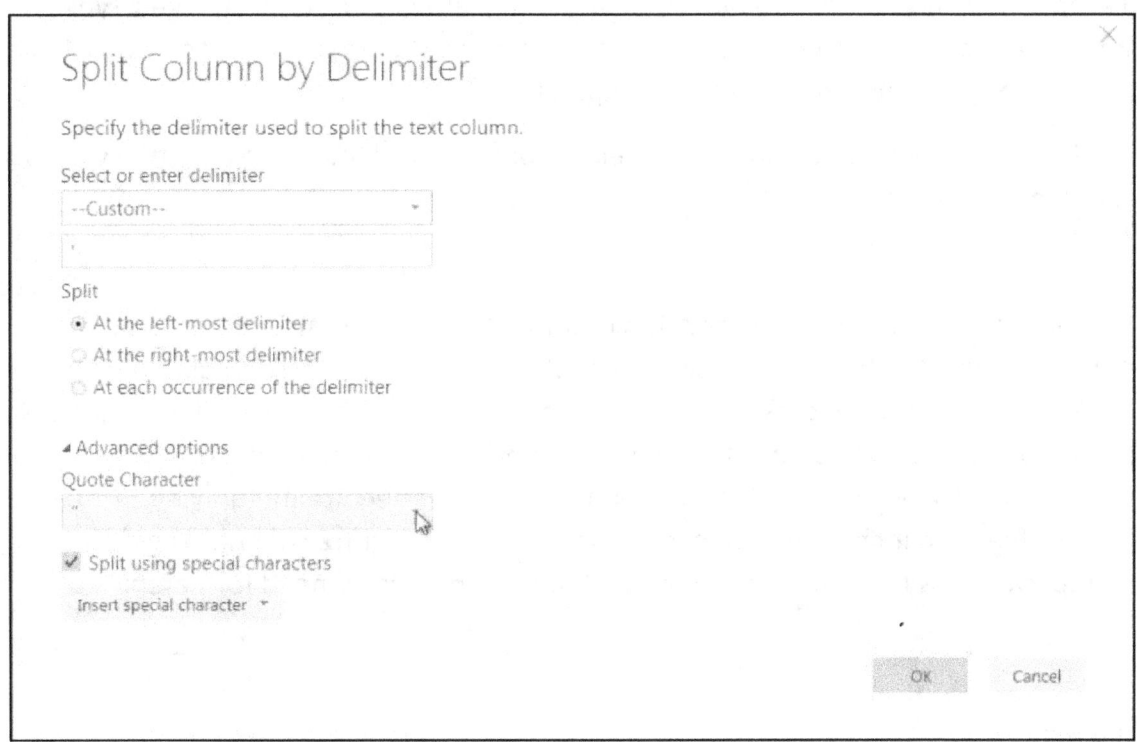

By coincidence, the quote character is the same as the symbol for inches; so, if we simply leave **Split using special character** turned on, when we click **OK**, we will up with two height columns: Height.1 And Height.2; and they will both contain numeric values.

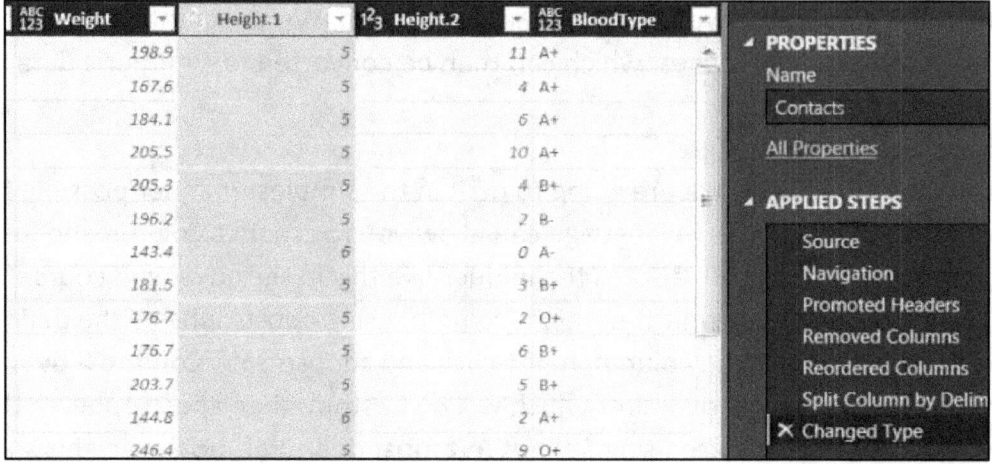

Although we performed only one step, Split by Delimiter, we ended up with two. Because we left the quote character option switched on, the quotation marks disappeared; and the Query Editor then automatically generated a Changed Type step to convert both columns to the whole number data type; which is exactly what we need. So, we can simply leave this in place.

Our final step will be to create a new Height column which combines the two values in Height.1 and Height.2.

## Using the Add Custom Columns Command

To create a new column, we click **Add Column > Custom Column**. Let us name the column "Height". (This does not cause a clash, as the original Height column no longer exists.) Then, we click in the formula box and, conveniently, we have a list of all the available columns; on which we can simply double-click to insert them into our formula. So, we double-click on Height.1; then, we need to multiply by 12 to convert feet into inches; and then, simply add on the Height.2 column. The multiplication will be done before the addition so there is no need for parentheses.

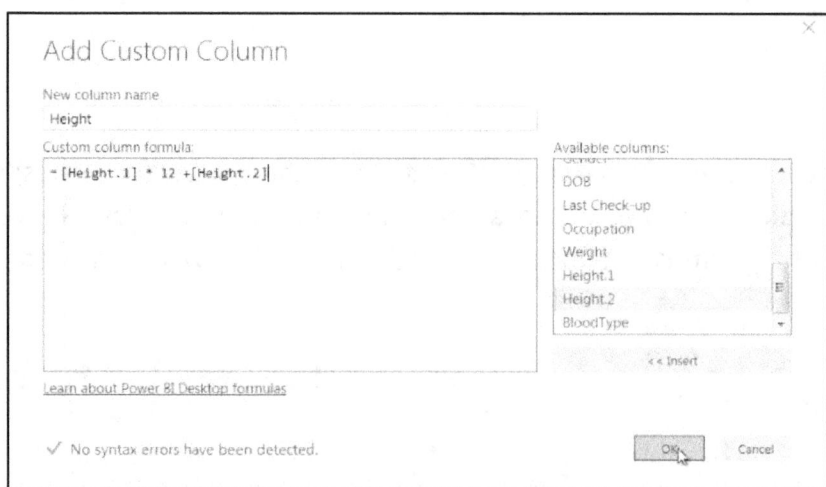

Click **OK**, and now we have the height in inches.

Although the new Height column was derived from Height.1 and Height.2, we no longer need them. If you are used to performing similar operations in Excel, you might think that Height depends on Height.1 and Height.2; but, in fact, they only needed to exist at the point where we created the new Height column. Having created this column, Height.1 and Height.2 are no longer necessary. So, we can highlight both, and use **Right-click > Remove Columns**; and the height column remains intact.

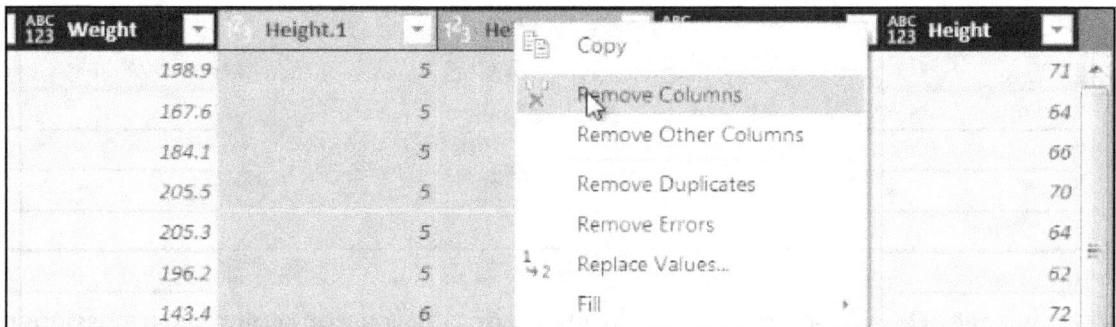

Now, we can move onto the creation of the BMI column. Click **Add Column > Custom Column**; and enter the name "BMI".

If you look in the training folder, inside 09-Creating Custom Columns, you will find the BMI conversion formula.

```
BMI conversion formula.txt - Notepad
File  Edit  Format  View  Help
BMI CALCULATION


IMPERIAL

  BMI = (Weight in Pounds / (Height in inches x Height in inches)) x 703


METRIC

  BMI = (Weight in Kilograms / (Height in Meters x Height in Meters))
```

We will be working in imperial; so, we take the weight in pounds and divide it by the square of height in inches; and then multiply the result by 703.

So, having clicked on **Add Column > Custom Column**, in the Custom Column dialog, enter the column name "BMI"; then enter the formula shown below, double-clicking on the appropriate column names in the column list as required.

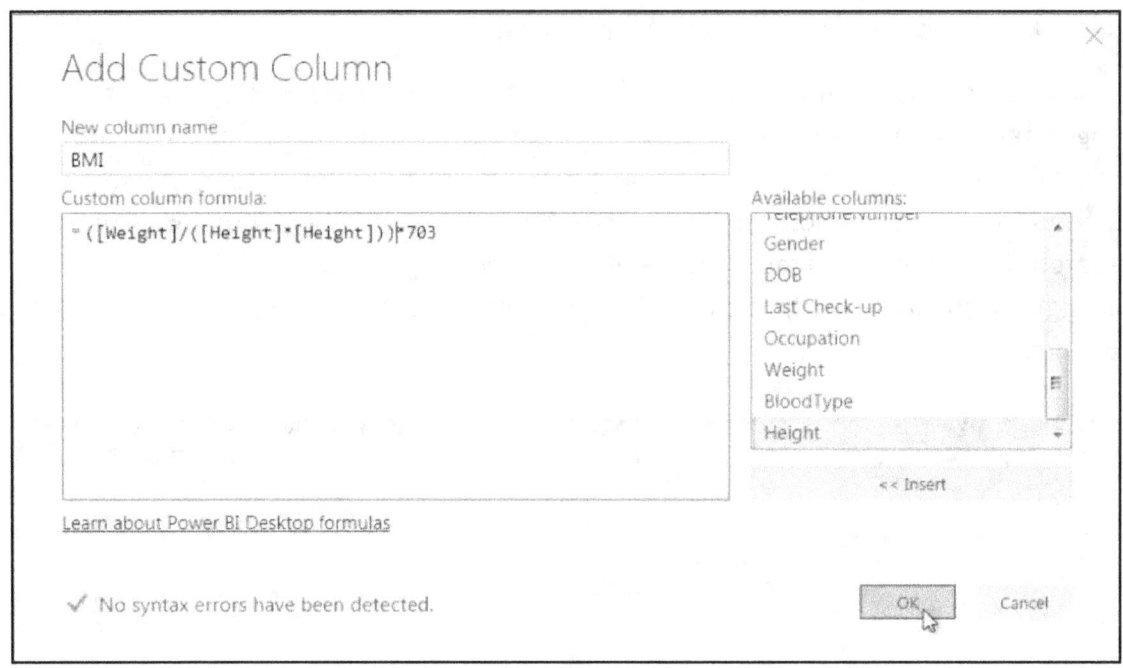

When we click **OK**, we see our new column. By default, custom columns are assigned the text data type, the final step will, therefore, be to convert the data type to a decimal number; then, we can convert the other columns which need to be converted:

Weight: whole number.

Date of Birth: date.

Last check up: date.

Credit card expiry: date.

That is our introduction to the creation of custom columns, when we move onto data modelling (in the next title in this series) we will encounter DAX calculated columns. Wherever possible, to improve performance, it is better to create custom columns in the Query Editor rather than as DAX calculated columns later, in the data modelling stage.

## Conclusion

The Query Editor provides several different ways of creating new columns, hence the presence of a Ribbon Tab named Add Column.

The Custom Column command is very useful for creating a new column derived from existing ones.

Columns used to create a new custom column can subsequently be removed without "breaking" the new column.

# Chapter 10: Append Queries

Power BI contains two very useful features for stitching together matching rows and columns of data: Append Queries and Merge Queries. In this chapter, we will look at Append Queries, which performs vertical stitching: combining rows of data, from separate queries, into one.

## Importing the Data

Let us begin by importing our data; this time we will be using CSV files, of which we need three, and which we will import in alphabetical order.

Click **Home > Get Data > Text/CSV**; then, in the exercises folder, open sub-folder "10-Append Queries"; and double-click "Leeds.csv "to import the file. Click on **Edit** to load the data into the Query Editor.

Next, from inside the Query Editor, Click **Home > New Source > Text/CSV**; double-click "Liverpool.csv" to import the file; and click **OK** to load the data into the Query Editor. Finally, repeat this process to load "Manchester.csv".

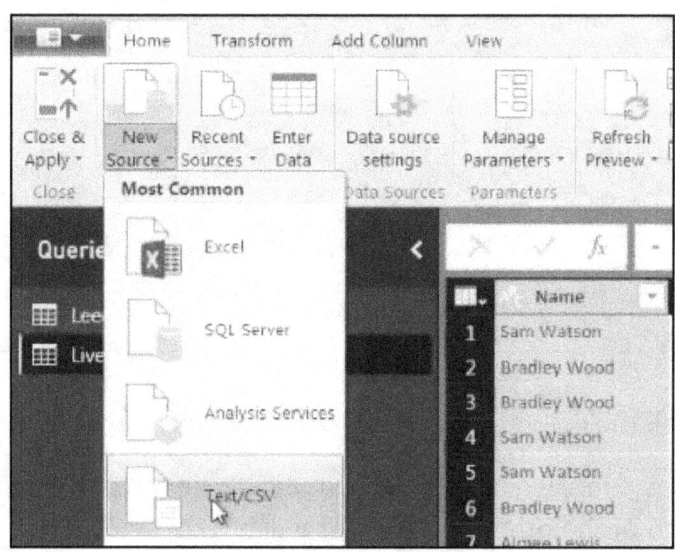

So, here we have three files which contain essentially the same type of data, and it is in these circumstances that one uses the Append Queries command. Append Queries will, basically, combine rows of data from separate queries into a single query.

## Removing the differences between columns

What we have is a fairly typical scenario; the data is essentially the same, but the columns are not identical. The typical first step is to remove the differences between the columns, so that we have, the same column headers and the same data types in all three queries.

In this example, we will be using Leeds as the definitive version, and we will modify the other two queries to match it. We have Name, Date, Amount and Category. So, in the Liverpool query, we will simply need to rename the columns; while, in the Manchester query, we will need to both rename columns and remove the Date Paid column which is not present in either the Leeds or Liverpool query.

As well as this, it will be useful to have an extra column which identifies the branch at which each person works; so, we will add a Branch column to each of the three queries.

Beginning with Leeds, we click on the **Add Column** Tab and click **Custom Column**. We will name the column "Branch" and, as our formula, we will simply enter the literal value "Leeds", which is text and, therefore, must be placed inside double quotes.

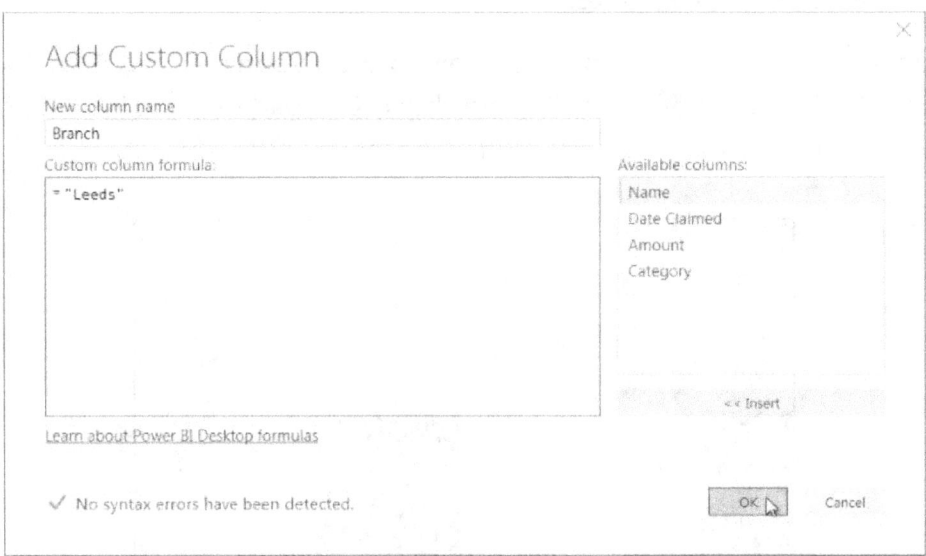

So, we now have all the columns we need for the Leeds query.

In the Applied Steps pane, we have an automatically generated Changed Type step; and, naturally, each of the other two queries will have a similar step; so, let us delete it and perform a single Change Type operation at the very end, once all the queries have been amalgamated into one.

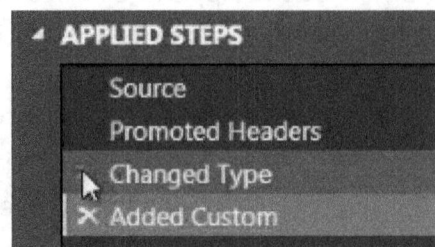

We can also change the name of the **Added Custom** step to **Add Branch Column**.

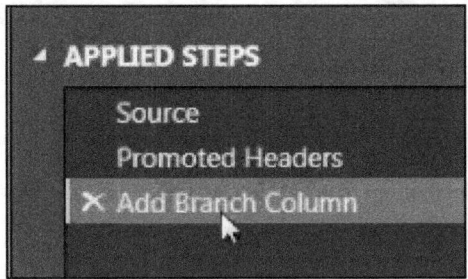

Let us now turn our attention to the Liverpool query. We need to ensure that the columns have the same names as the columns in the Leeds query. Hence, we need to change "Date" to "Date Claimed" and "Category" to "Description". This is just a case of double-clicking on the existing column header and modifying it.

Then we can add the branch column like we did in with Leeds. (In the following illustration, we have also changed the order of the columns to match that of the Leeds query; but this step is optional.

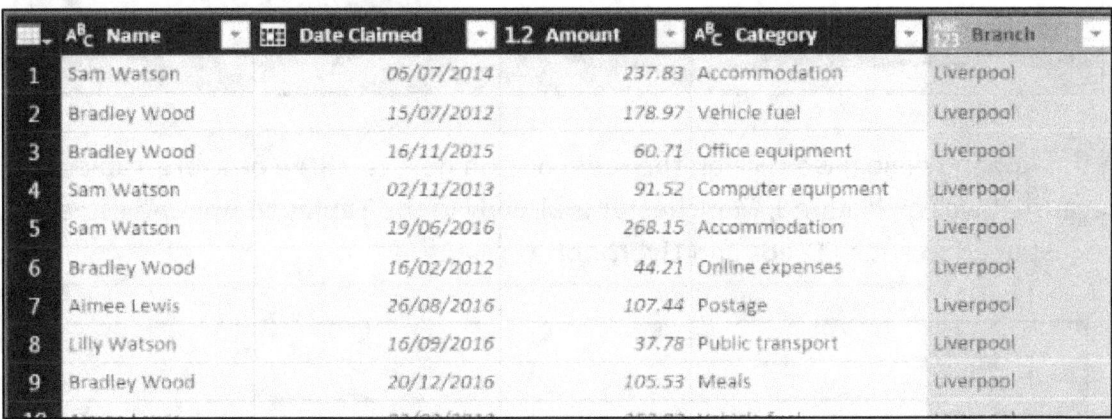

Tidy up the steps by removing the Changed Type and change the **Added Custom** to **Add Branch Column**.

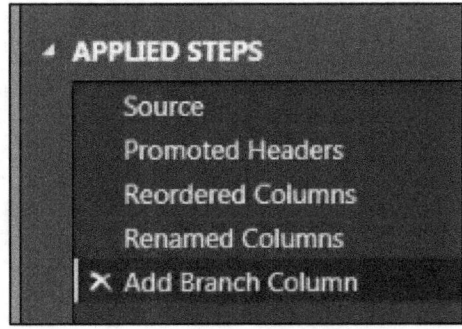

Finally, in the Manchester query, we have an extra column which is not present in the others; so, we can **Right-click** on the column header and choose **Remove**. And, as before, we will create a custom column, lose the change type and rename the **Added Custom** step as **Add Branch Column**.

## Using Append Queries as New

Now that we have parity between all the custom queries, we can go across to the Home Tab and in **Append Queries** dropdown, we can either use **Append Queries** or **Append Queries as New. Append Queries** will modify one of the existing queries in creating the new one; whereas **Append Queries as New** will create a completely new query, leaving the original queries intact. So, let us use **Append Queries as New**.

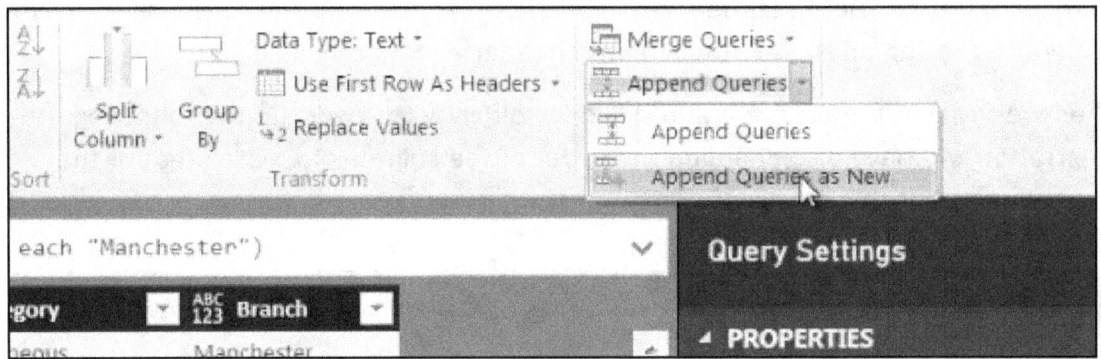

In the Append dialog, we click on the radio button next to **Three or More Tables**. Because it was highlighted, **Manchester** is already in the **Tables to Append** list; so, we just need to add in **Leeds** and **Liverpool**.

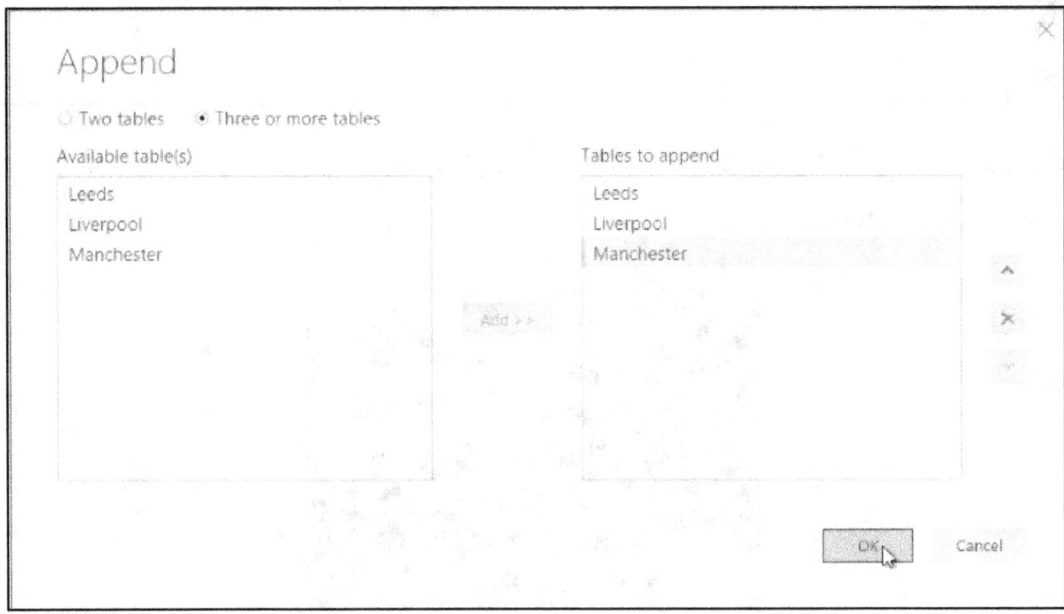

When we click **OK**, having amalgamated all our data into one query, we cab rename the new query "North".

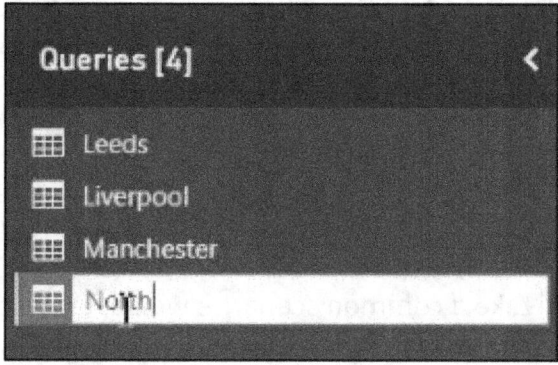

This would also be the logical time to change data types. Date Claimed needs to be a **Date** and Amount needs to be currency, i.e., **Fixed decimal number**.

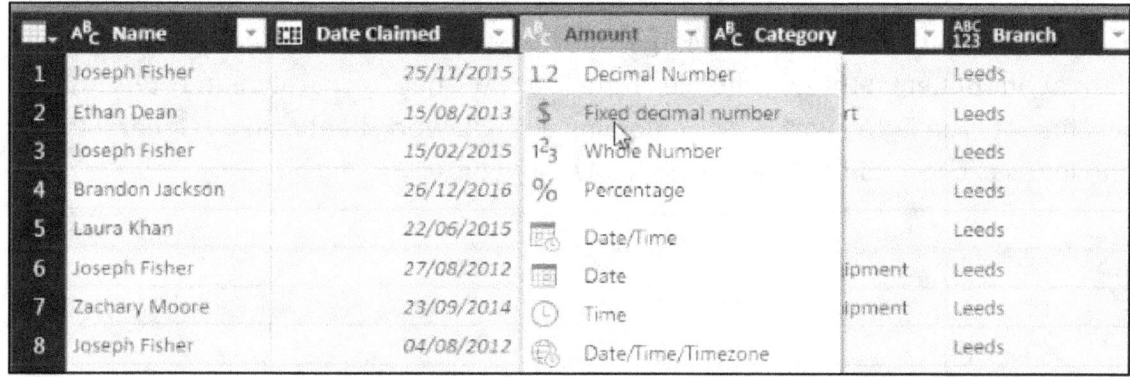

## Conclusion

The Append queries as new command will create a new query which contains all the rows in several original queries.

For the command to produce useful results, all the original queries should have the same columns and the column headings must all be identical.

## Chapter 11: Merge Queries

In the last chapter, we looked at how Append Queries can be used to (vertically) stitch together rows of data from different queries. In this chapter, we will look at its "partner in crime", Merge Queries, which is used to (horizontally) stitch together columns of data.

Merge Queries is used where you have two data source which have rows in common; whereas Append Queries is used when you have two or more data sources which have columns in common.

In this example, we will take a common scenario: we have two data sources which contain information about the same group (in this case, a group of subscribers to a newsletter). The reason that the information exists as two separate sources is that one source contains standard information, while the other contains slightly more sensitive data.

We will begin by connecting to our data sources, both of which are Excel files. You will find them in sub-folder "11-Merge Queries". What we have, in this scenario, is data about patients; thus, in the file "Data.xlsx", we have general data. Let us import this first. It is an Excel workbook containing a single worksheet called "General Data"; and let us click on **Edit** to load it into the Query Editor.

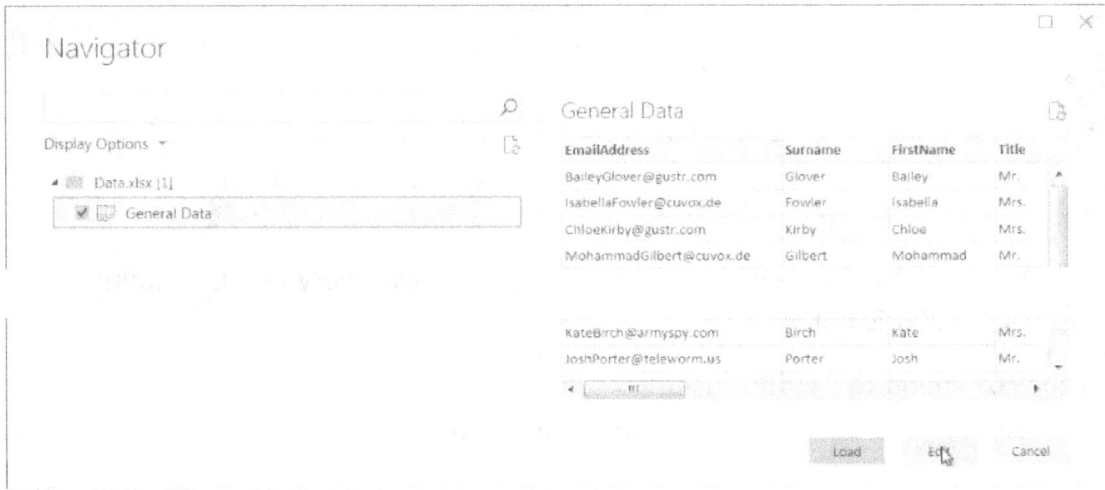

Then we can grab the second dataset, by clicking **Home > New Source > Excel**; and, this time, importing "Personal.xlsx".

We now need to bring together all the data in these two reports. The two datasets contain data about the same individuals, identified by the email address column which is found in both datasets. Having a common column in both queries is a requirement when using the Merge Queries command.

## Using Merge Queries as New

As with the Append Queries command, you have the choice of either merging into one of the original queries; or, creating a completely new query, which merges the two original queries together. You will usually find that the latter approach is more useful. So, let us highlight General Data query, and, in the Home Tab, above Append Queries, you will find Merge Queries; and, again, we have both **Merge Queries** and **Merge Queries as New**, which is the one that we want.

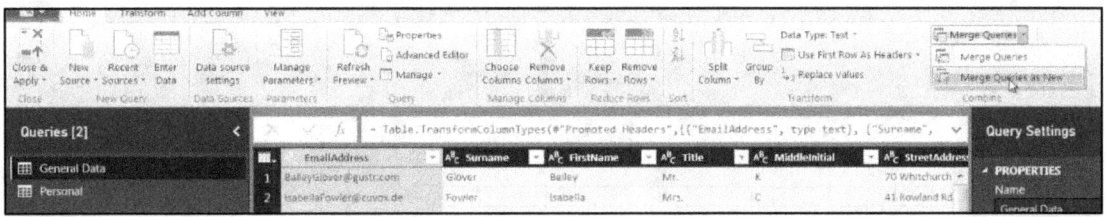

When the Merge dialog appears, we can see that our first table, General Data, is already highlighted; since we highlighted it before using the **Merge Queries as New** command. So, now we need to specify that email address is the column which we want to use for matching, and we do this simply by clicking on the column.

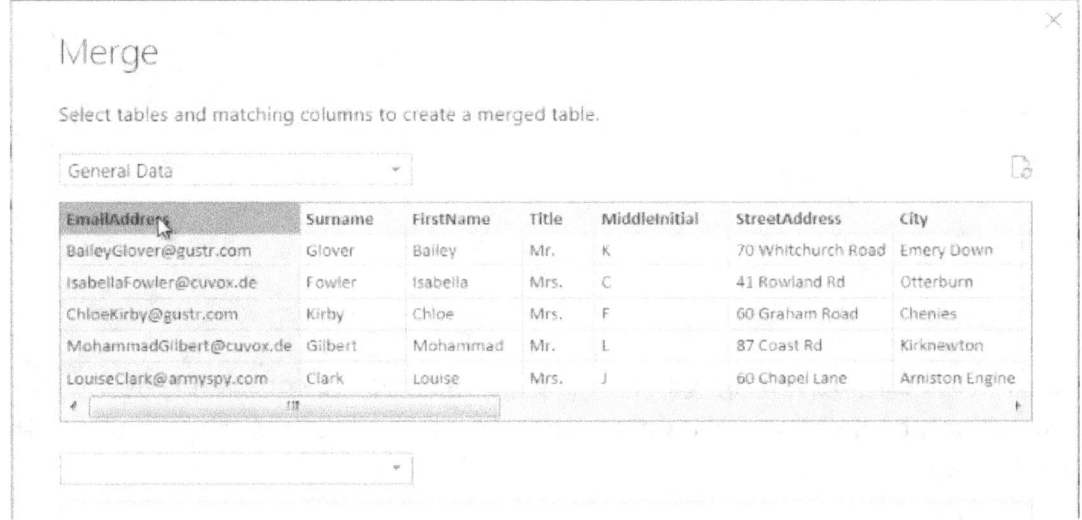

We can specify our second Table which, of course, is Personal; and we specify that Email is the matching column as before.

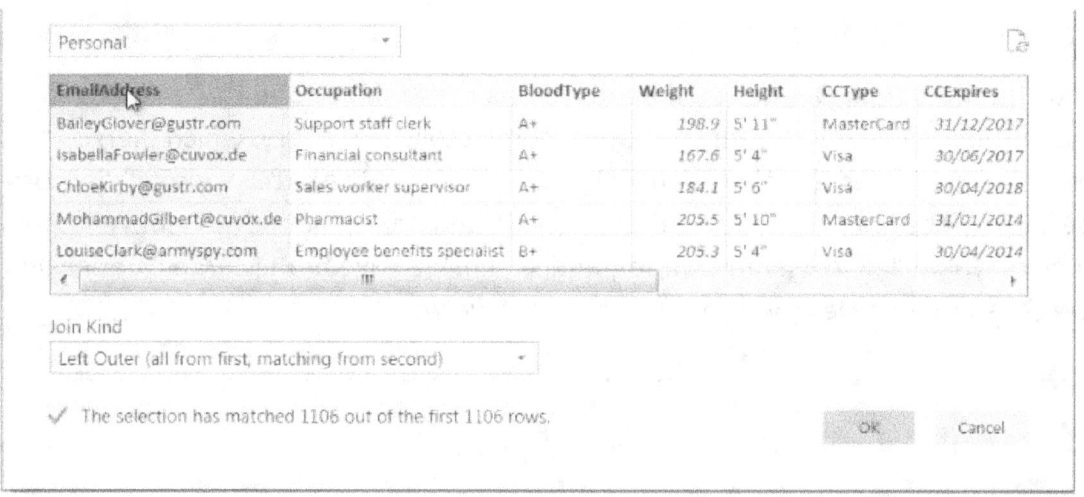

## Specifying the Join Kind

We then have all the possible ways of joining the two datasets; and you will probably recognise these options as being identical to SQL joins. Let us say that, in our scenario, we only want the matching columns from both datasets. Thus, we choose **Inner (only matching rows)**.

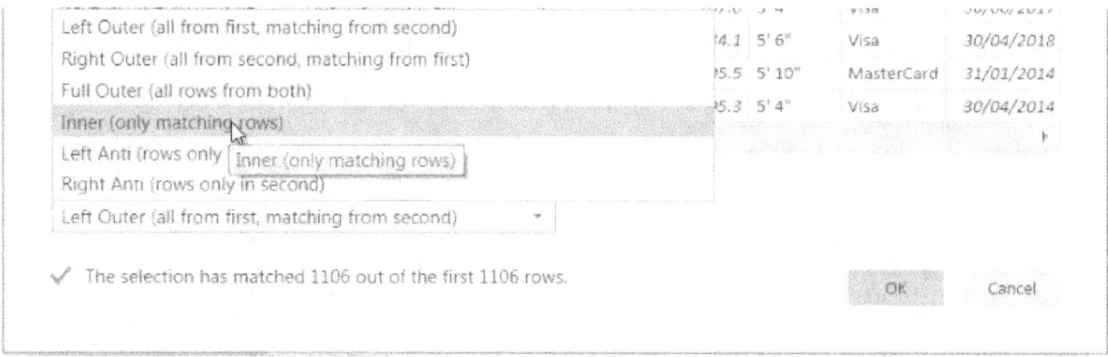

When we click **OK**, the settings we have chosen will create a completely new query which will only contain rows of data where the same email address is found in both original queries.

Our new query is created, and, at first glance, it only appears to contain the information from General Data. However, if we scroll all the way to the right, we find an additional, binary column, called simply "NewColumn", and containing the data from Personal Data. Also, we can see several columns which contain no data at all. Simply highlight all of these (click on the first, Shift-click on the last) and then **Right-click > Remove Columns**.

Finally, we need to click on the Expand button, on the right of the "NewColumn" column, to get access to all the other columns from the Personal query. We can begin by deselecting all columns and just activating the ones which we want to add to this query. Email address we already have. We need Occupation, Blood Type, Weight, Height, Credit Card Type and Credit Card Expiry. Once again, several blank columns are being picked up from the Excel worksheet, which we can also ignore. The final thing we need to do is to deactivate the option **Use original column name as prefix**, since this is only useful when avoiding clashes in column names.

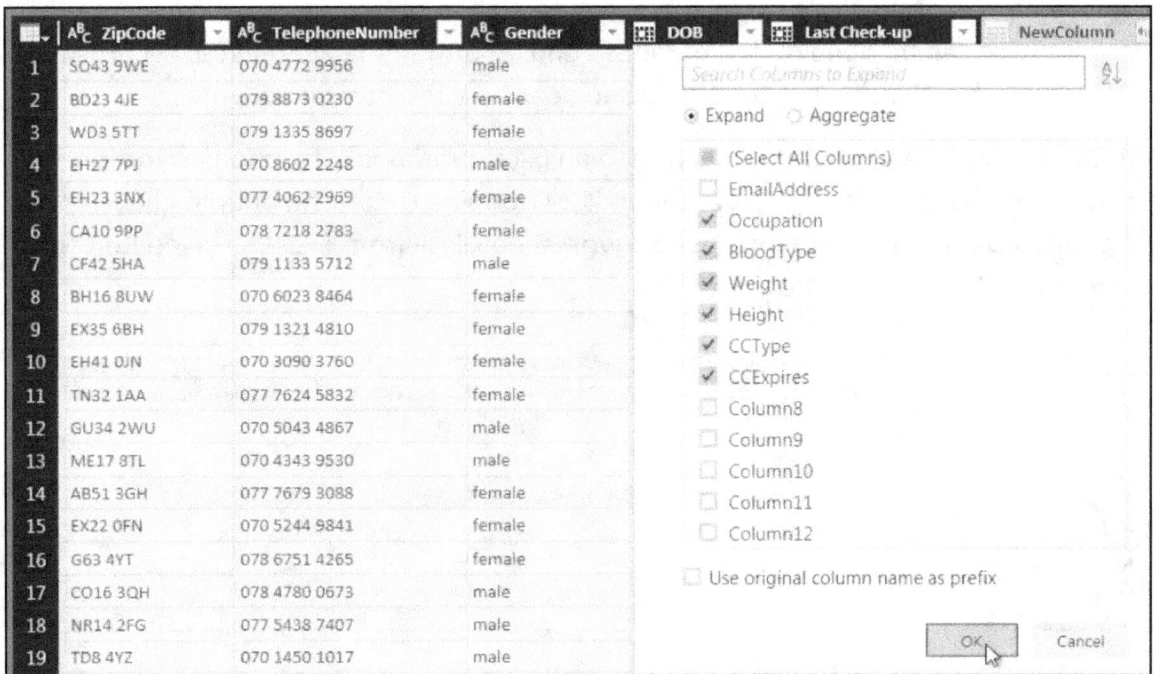

When we click **OK**, we have all the personal columns added to our query, and we can then carry out any further transformations which our dataset requires.

## Conclusion

As you can see the Append Queries and Merge Queries command work in very similar ways.

The Append Queries command amalgamates rows of data and Merge Queries amalgamates columns of data.

# Chapter 12: Grouping Data

## Benefits of Grouping Data

When you are connecting to a data source which has lots of rows of data, more rows than you need; it is often useful to aggregate the data prior to import it. The Query Editor's **Group by** command allows you to do this.

This feature is particularly useful when connecting to database servers; because the aggregation can be done on the database end, and then the aggregated records are sent through to Power BI. Let us have a look at how the command works.

In this example, we will be connecting to an Excel workbook; so, choose **Home > Get Data > Excel** and navigate to sub-folder "12-Grouping Data" and double-click on "All Expenses Data.xlsx". This contains raw worksheet data from Excel. Click on **Edit** to load it into the Query Editor.

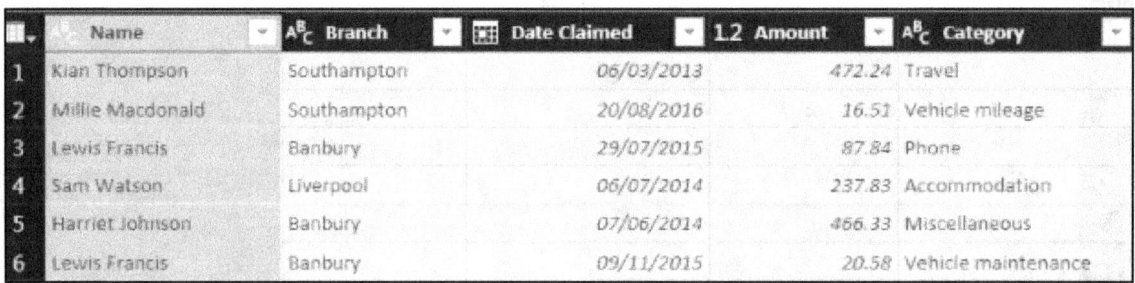

Our data gives details of every single expense claim made by all our account handlers; so, if we do not need to have that level of granularity, if it is sufficient to know the total claimed by each account handler; then we can group this data by the Name column. Thus, we will have one row for each individual and the amount they have claimed, and this will be the starting point for our dataset.

## Adding Groupings

To use this feature, simply highlight the **Name** column then click on **Home > Group by**. Since **Name** was highlighted, it is shown as the **Group by** column. However, we can add as many groupings as we like; and, in this example, we can click on **Add grouping** and add the **Branch** column without introducing any further granularity to our dataset; because each individual works for a specific branch, adding the **Branch** will not generate any extra records in the dataset.

If we add the Date Claimed or the Category, this would introduce further granularity; which is exactly what we are trying to avoid.

## Adding Aggregations

Next, we can think about aggregation. Click **Add aggregation**; and let us call the new column **Amount**; and the operation that we want is the **Sum** of the **Amount** column.

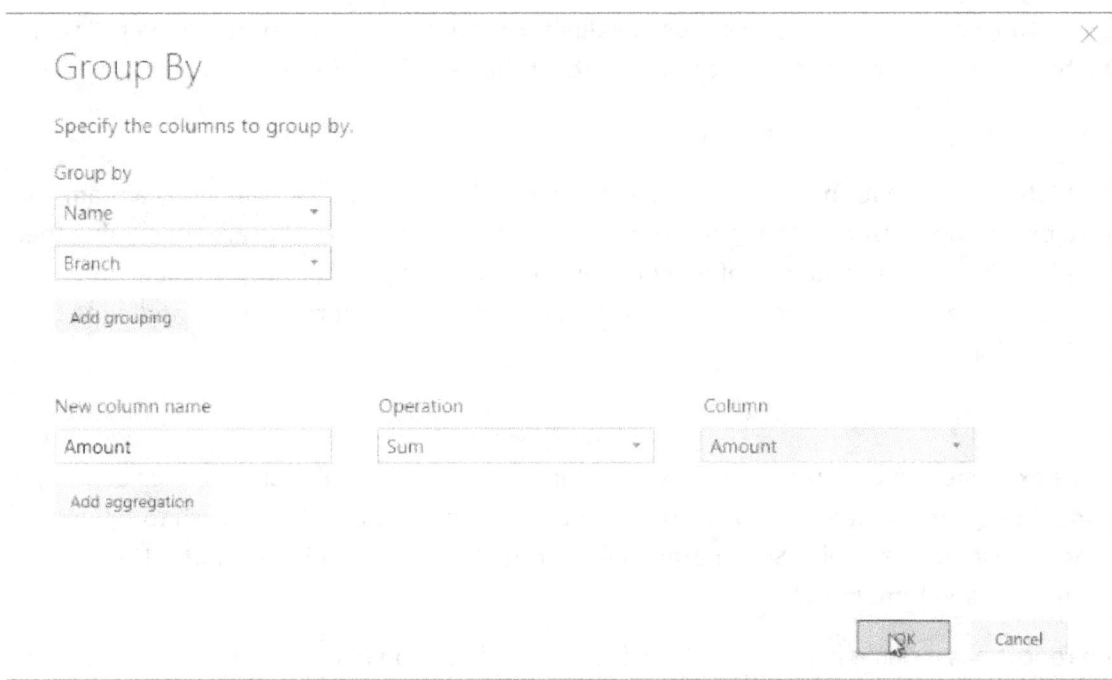

When we click **OK**, we can see that we now have only one row for each individual, the name of the branch at which they work, and the total amount they claimed.

## Conclusion

The Group by command is particularly useful where you have millions of rows of data in the original dataset, but where the full granularity of that data is not required in your Power BI report.

It is also a useful trade-off when you are looking to improve performance and know that importing millions of rows of data will slow response time when users interact with your reports.

# Chapter 13: Power Query Parameters and Templates

Query Parameters allow you to make the content of a report dependent on one or more parameter values. Often used in conjunction with parameters, templates allow you to export a complete report without including any data. When you open a template in Power BI Desktop, you will be asked to supply a value for each defined parameter. Power BI then creates a new report based upon the contents of the template file.

## Benefits of parameters and templates

Templates are a great time-saver and can be utilized both by a single user or by a team, with more experienced users creating the templates and less experienced users consuming them. Templates are also a great way of avoiding duplication of effort and preventing errors and omissions. They also allow you to standardize key aspects of reports, from branding to data manipulation.

## Overview of Our Example

In this example, we will create a mini sales reporting template which shows sales of a single product range made at a particular branch of a fictitious company. If you wish to follow along, please open the file "Single Branch & Product Range.pbix" in the folder "13-Parameters and templates".

The report has a single page, called "Products", which is shown in the following illustration.

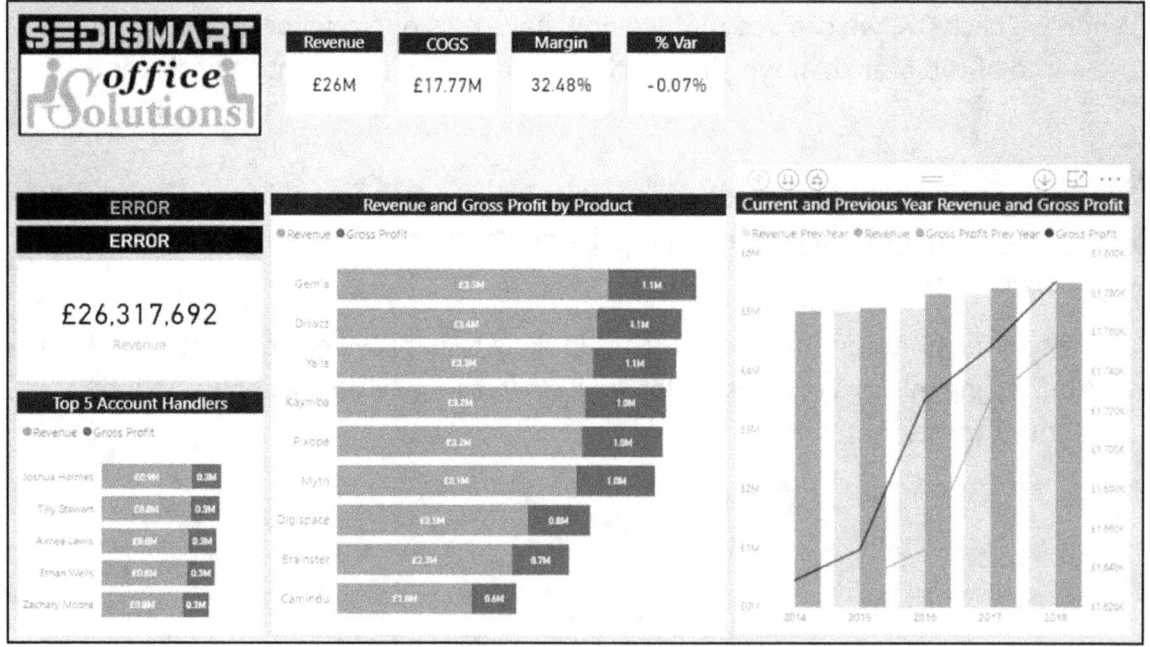

## Creating Dynamic Titles

On the left of the screen are two cards; as shown in the illustrations above, both will initially display the word "Error". However, when the template is used, the top card will display the product range, while the second will display the branch, as shown below.

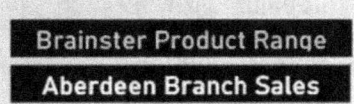

When creating dynamic titles in templates, best practice is to ensure that they always display an error or warning until suitable values are supplied for each parameter. This is done by creating DAX measures which use a conditional statement.

We will not be discussing DAX until the next title in the series. However, it is probable that you are already aware of DAX (or, if not, of Excel IF statements) and will find the following statements fairly easy to follow.

The formula for generating the Branch name is as follows:

```
Title Branch =
IF (
    DISTINCTCOUNT ( SalesData[Branch]) = 1 && DISTINCTCOUNT (
SalesData[Product Range] ) = 1,
    SELECTEDVALUE (SalesData[Branch] ) & " Branch Sales",
    "ERROR"
)
```

And here is the one for generating the Product Range:

```
Title Product Range =
IF (
    DISTINCTCOUNT ( SalesData[Branch]) = 1 && DISTINCTCOUNT (
SalesData[Product Range] ) = 1,
    SELECTEDVALUE ( SalesData[Product Range]) & " Product
Range",
    "ERROR"
)
```

Let us briefly examine the DAX syntax.

First, we use the DISTINCTCOUNT function in a Boolean test to verify whether both the Staff[Branch] and Products[Product Range] columns contain one distinct value each. If both do contain unique values, then our formula outputs:

```
MIN ( Staff[Branch] ) & " Branch Sales"
```
Or

```
MIN ( Products[Product Range] ) & " Product Range"
```

(The factor which will cause the DISTINCTCOUNT of the Branch and Product Range columns to return one is the implementation of two parameters as filters: one on each of the two columns.)

The MIN function will of course return the first element in the column and, since we have verified that there is only value in that column, MIN must, therefore, return the value which we need. We then concatenate this value with " Branch Sales" or " Product Range".

If our IF statements produce a negative result (as is now the case), our formulas both output the word **"ERROR"**.

## Creating parameters

Parameters are created in Power BI Desktop, using the Query Editor window (**Home > Edit Queries**). In the Query Editor, we choose **Home > Manage Parameters > New Parameter**.

### Name and Description

In the dialog which appears, we can create new parameters and add metadata. Let us begin by entering the **Name** "Product Range" and the **Description** "Choose the Product Range which will be the focus of this report.".

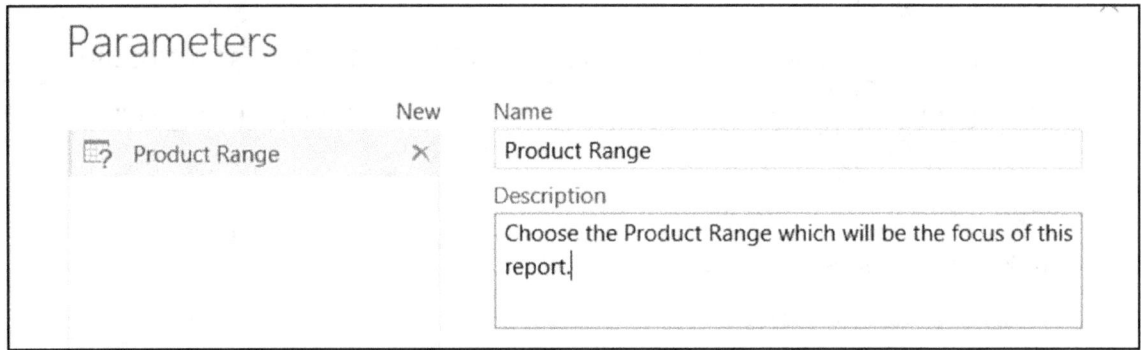

The Description will be displayed next to the parameter name each time the template is used. It is very important since it guides the user to provide the correct value for the parameter.

### Optional or Required

Next, we can specify whether the parameter is optional or whether a value must be specified. In this example, we want the parameter to be obligatory; so, we choose **Required**.

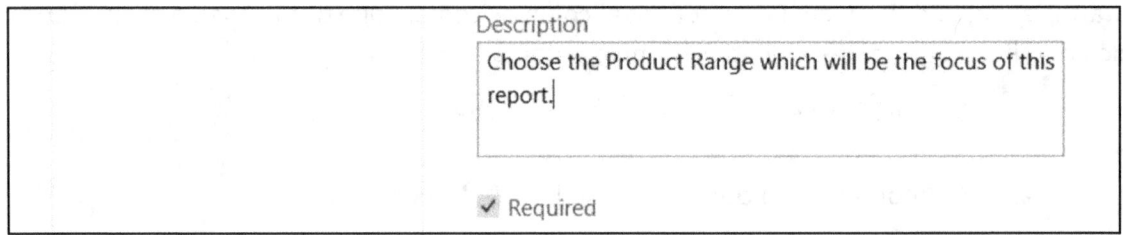

Parameter Type

The **Parameter Type** setting allows us to specify the data type of the parameter value; so, here, we choose **Text**.

Any

Decimal Number

Date/Time

Date

Time

Date/Time/Timezone

Duration

Text

True/False

Binary

Suggested Values

In addition to the Data Type, we can apply further restrictions to the permitted parameter values. Since we have a limited number of product ranges, let us set this option to **List of Values**.

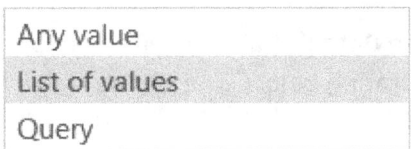

Any value

List of values

Query

Having chosen this option, you will be presented with a grid into which you can either enter or paste your list. Unless the list is very short, you will normally find the latter option preferable. If the information exists in a database, you can use a SQL query to generate a sorted unique list. In this example, we will use Excel.

Open the file called "Sales_Data.xlsx" in the "13-Parameters and templates" folder. Activate the worksheet tab named "PRODS"; select the product range names in cells C2 to C67 and copy them to a new blank workbook. Use Data > Remove Duplicates and Data > Sort; then, select and copy the resulting nine product range names.

Finally, return to the Power BI Query Editor and paste the values into the grid below the **List of Values** option.

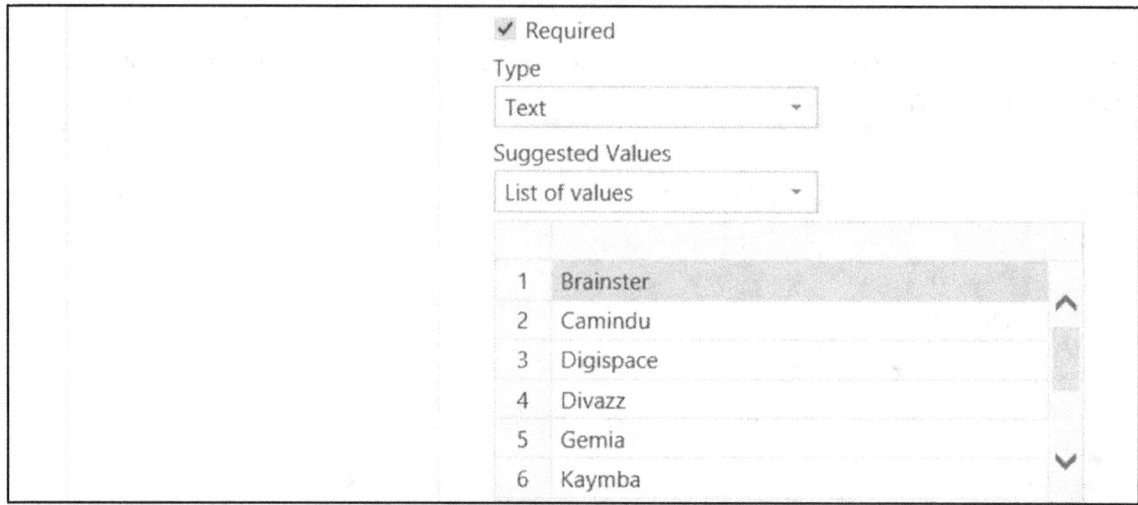

### Default Value vs Current Value

The final two options in the Parameters dialog allow you to specify an optional **Default Value** and an obligatory **Current Value**. Although it depends on the circumstance, default values are often a bad idea since they encourage users to accept the default without realizing that they have the option of making another choice.

This Current Value setting allows you to choose or enter a parameter value for immediate use. The value specified will determine the data returned by any query in which the parameter is implemented.

In this example, let us leave the **Default Value** blank and choose any value from the **Current Value** drop-down. (In the illustration below, The **Gemia** range has been chosen.)

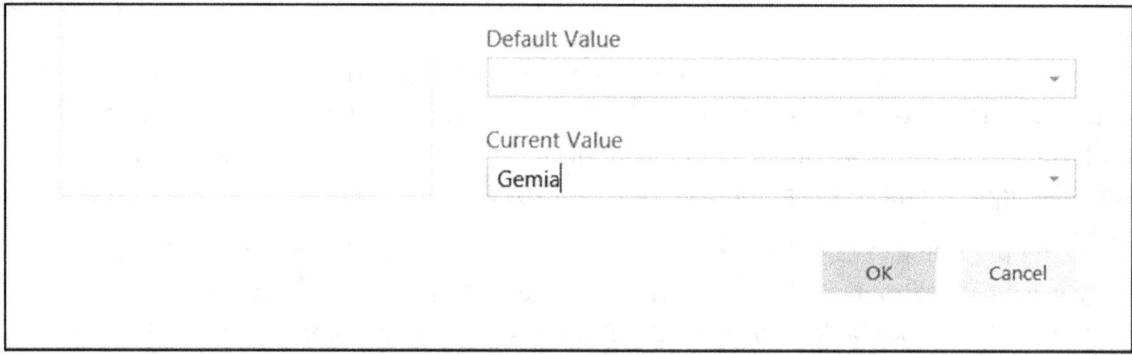

Before clicking the **OK** button, you can create as many parameters as you need. To create a second parameter, simply click the New button in the top left of the dialog.

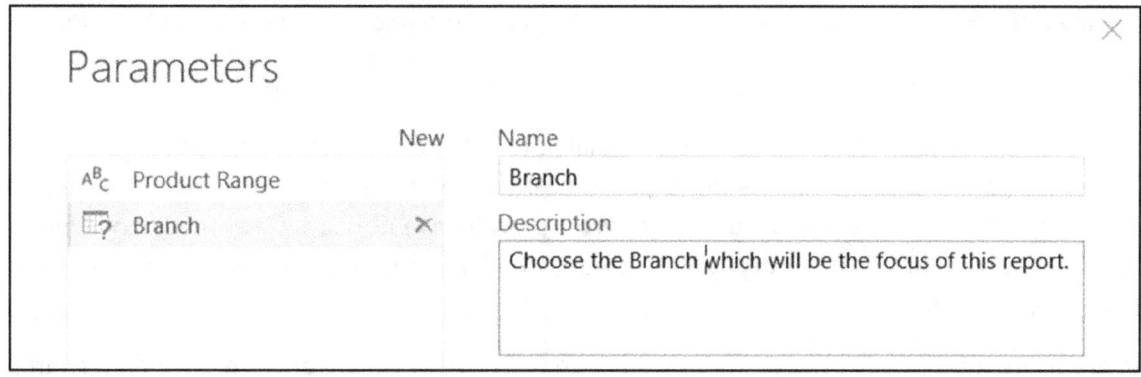

For our second parameter, let us enter the **Name** "Branch" and the **Description** "Choose the Branch which will be the focus of this report.".

Next, using the techniques outlined above, create a text parameter which uses a list of values. (Create and copy the list from the Branch column of the "STFF" worksheet in "13-Parameters and templates".)

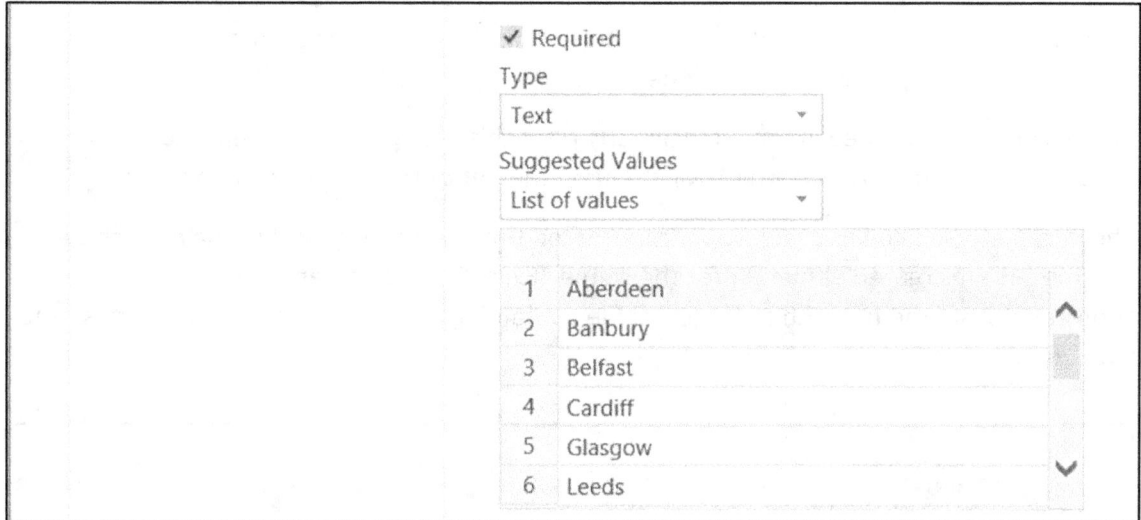

Leave the **Default Value** blank and choose any value from the **Current Value** drop-down. (In the illustration below, The **London** branch has been chosen.)

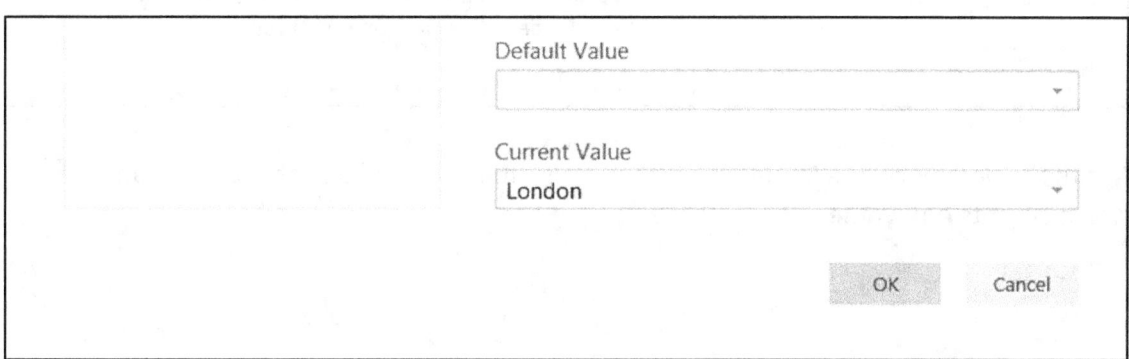

Having defined our two parameters, let us click **OK** and move on to their implementation.

## Creating Parameters on the Fly

As well as going straight to the Parameters dialog to create parameters, it is possible to create (and simultaneously implement) parameters on the fly. To illustrate this technique, let us use a parameter to fix our broken query. You will have noticed, on entering the Query Editor, that the Sales_Data query used to create the dataset is displaying the triangular data source error icon.

If you have been using Power BI for a while, you will have probably encountered data source errors before. Since the dataset is connected to a file source, when the PBIX file is opened on a different machine, the path to the file will no longer be the same.

If we parameterize a data source, then we can update all the queries using that data source simply by specifying a different parameter value.

In the Query Editor, let us highlight the Sales_Data query, and in the Applied Steps dialog, double-click on the **Source** step to display Excel dialog. Clicking the **Advanced** radio button to split the file path into multiple parts is a very useful option and is often used in conjunction with parameters. However, in this example, let us use a parameter to replace the entire file path; so, we will leave the **Basic** option selected.

We can now create a new parameter directly from this dialogue by choosing **New Parameter** from the drop-down (**ABC**) menu on the left of the **File Path** dialog.

The Parameters dialog appears, superimposed on the Excel dialog, and displaying the two parameters we created earlier. Enter the Name "Excel Sales Data" and the Description "Copy and paste the full path to the Excel file containing the sales data. (The path must end with .xlsx.)".

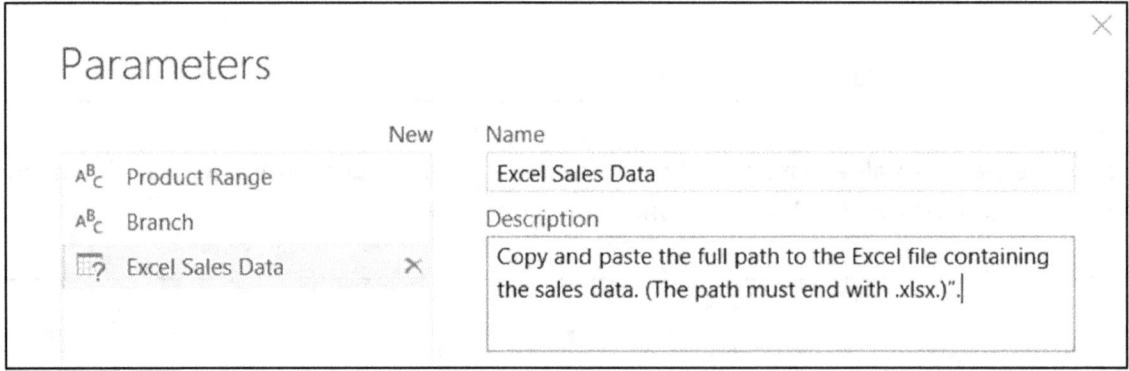

Again, the parameter is a **Required** one and, this time, we need a simple text parameter which accepts **Any Value**.

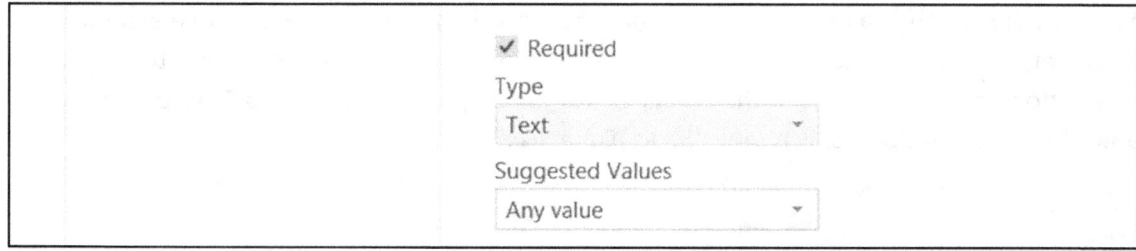

Finally, copy and paste the full path to the file "13-Parameters and templates \Sales_Data.xlsx", on your computer, into the **Current Value** field and click the **OK** button.

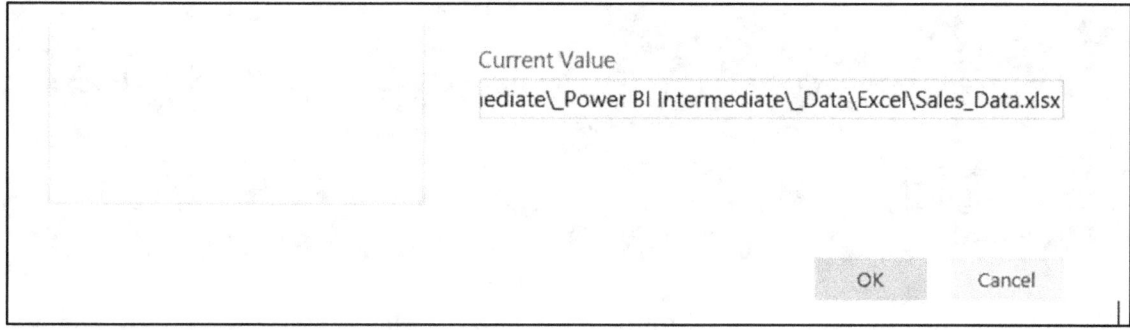

Back in the Excel dialog, your newly-created parameter will automatically have replaced the static value in the **File Path** field.

 Click **OK** and the data error on the Sales_Data query will have disappeared.

## Updating a Data Source via a Parameter

Now that our query uses the Excel Sales Data parameter as its data source, let us examine the mechanism for updating the data source via this parameter. In the source code folder, simply change the name of the Excel file from "Sales_Data.xlsx" to "Sales_Data2.xlsx". Now return to Power BI and click on **Home > Refresh Preview > Refresh All**.

Not surprisingly, the Sales_Data query again displays the triangular data source error icon. However, to fix the broken query, all we now need to do is edit a single parameter. In the Navigation pane, on the left of the Query Editor, highlight the **Excel Sales Data** parameter and the **Current Value** box, change "Sales_Data.xlsx" to "Sales_Data2.xlsx".

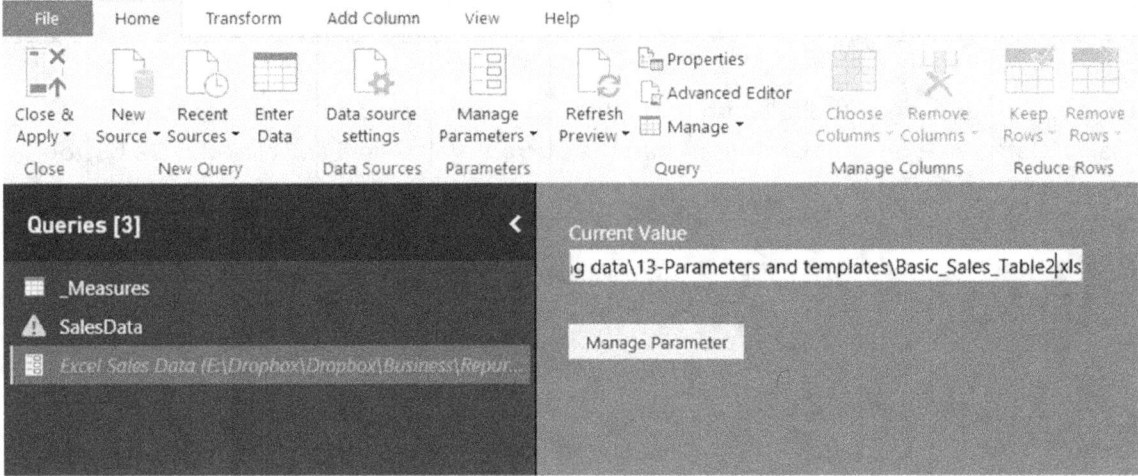

Naturally, as you can imagine, this feature becomes really useful when you have several queries all based on the same data source. Simply updating the value associated with the parameter updates all the queries which use that data source.

## Parameterizing Filter Operations

We now need to use our Product Range and Branch parameters to filter the rows displayed. Let us begin with the Products column.

In the Queries pane, highlight the Sales_Data query, then click on the filter arrow next to the **Product Range** column. Ignoring the check boxes, click on **Text Filters > Equals**.

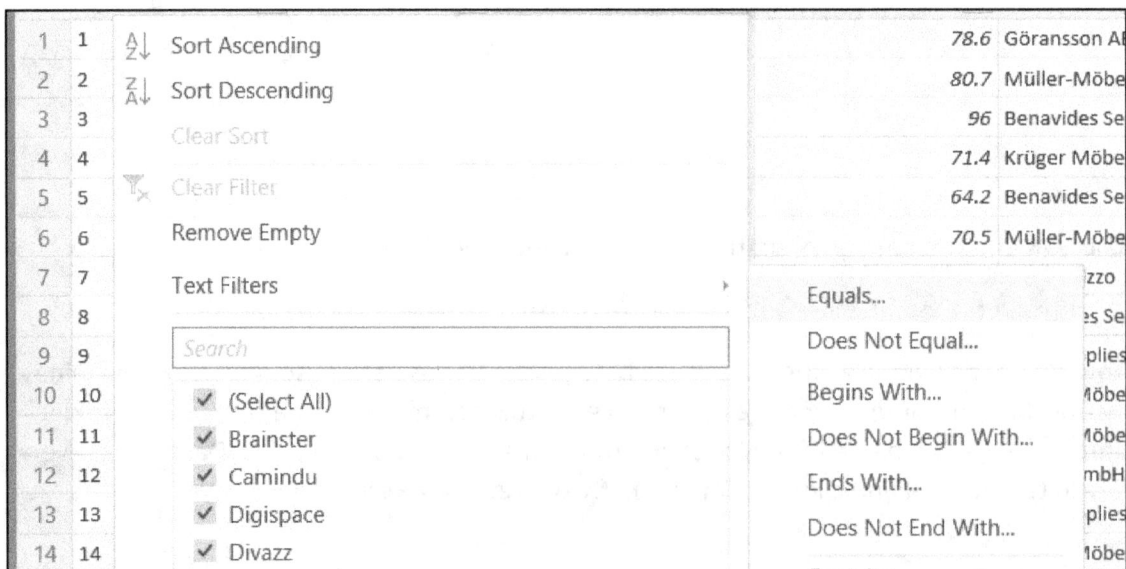

When the Filter Rows dialog pops up, choose **Parameter** from the drop-down next to **Keep Rows where Product Range Equals**. Then, choose the Product Range parameter from the Parameters drop-down.

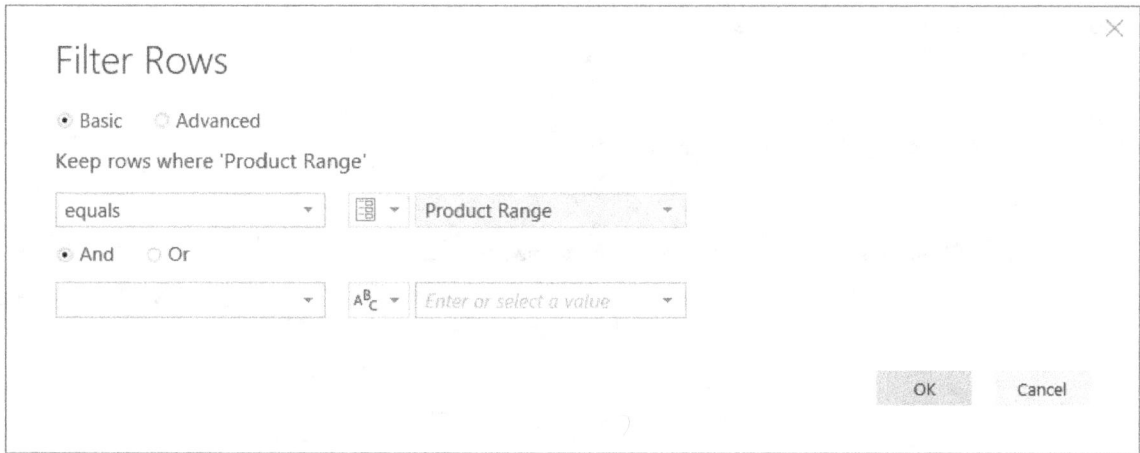

Repeat this same process to use the Branch parameter to filter the Branch column, using the Branch parameter you created earlier.

That completes our filtering operations. The filters applied to the Branch and Product Range columns will now be used to determine which rows in the Sales_Data table are loaded into the data model.

To see the effect of our filters, click **File > Close & Apply**. The error messages in our two cards should now have been replaced with "Gemia Product Range" and "London Branch Sales" (or something similar, depending on your earlier choices).

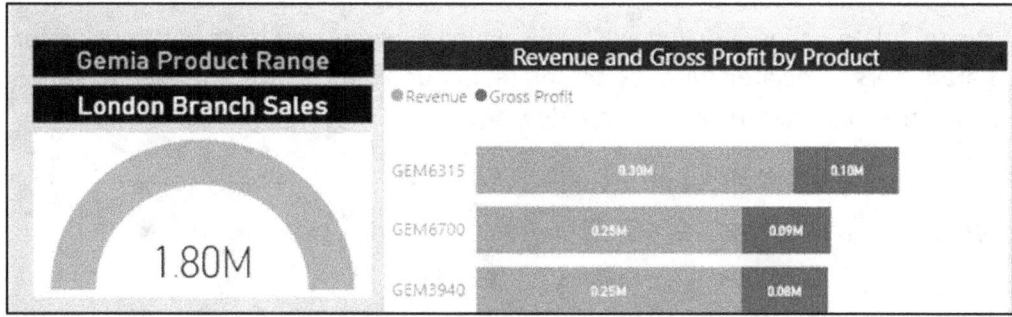

That completes our creation of the content of our template. Before we create the template itself, let us save our changes to the PBIX file.

## Creating a Template

Power BI's templates feature allows you to export a Power BI Desktop report (.PBIX) as a template (.PBIT) from which you can repeatedly generate new Power BI Desktop reports. A Power BI Report Template holds the query definitions, parameters, report pages and contents, and the data model definition. In short, it can be a fully-fledged Power BI report.

However, the template itself does not contain any data; so, template file sizes are usually very small.

To convert a report into a Power BI template, click **File > Export > Power BI Template** to display the Export a Template dialog.

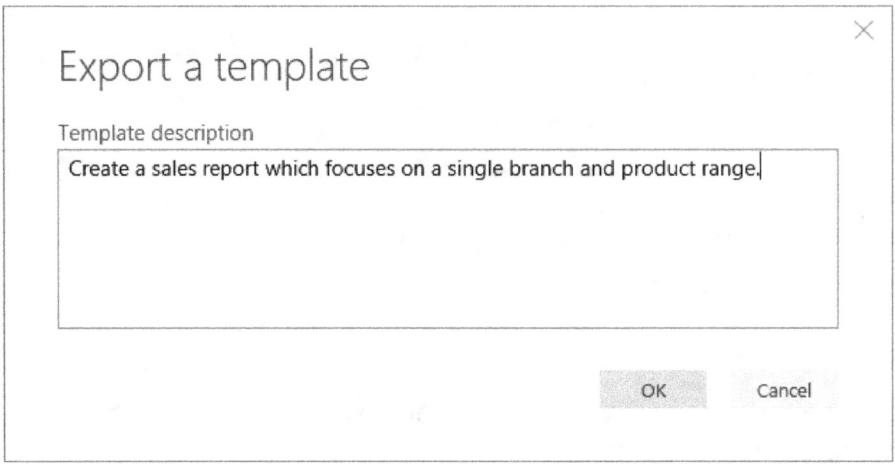

Enter a description for the template, click **OK**, specify a file name and location and click **Save**. (The file will be saved with a ".pbit" extension.)

## Using a Template

To use a Power BI Report Template, click **File > Import > Power BI Template**; or, double-click a PBIT file, in Windows or File Explorer, to open it. Both actions will create an untitled copy of the original template.

When the template opens, a dialog will be displayed allowing you to specify a value for each of the parameters associated with the template. In our example, we will need to supply a value of all three parameters, as shown below.

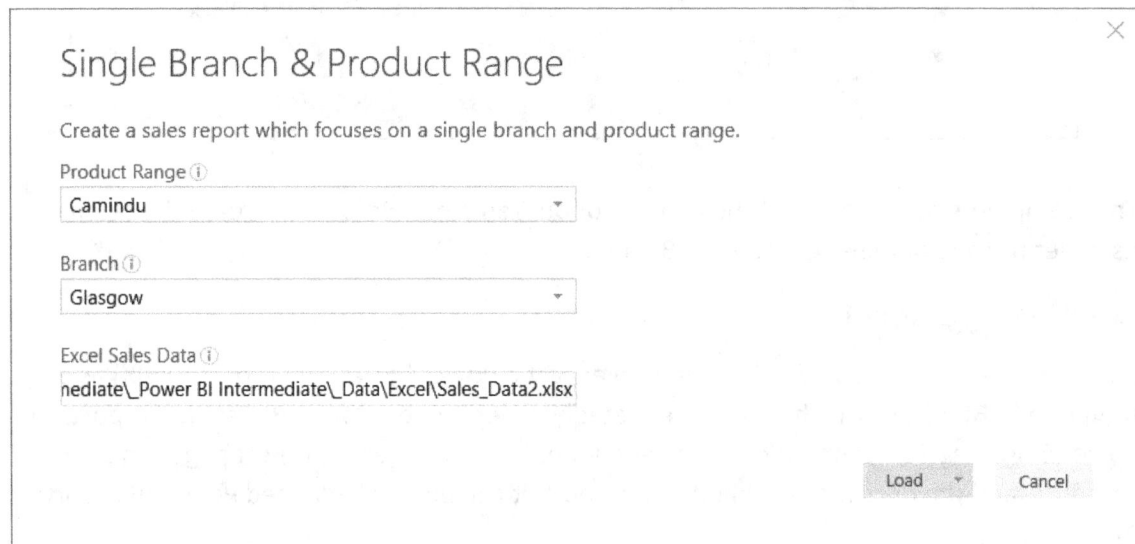

When we click load, a new PBIX file will be created, the report queries will run, the data model will be created and the report pages, containing all the original visuals, will be generated. And we can repeat this process as many times as we need to, entering different values each time for the various parameters.

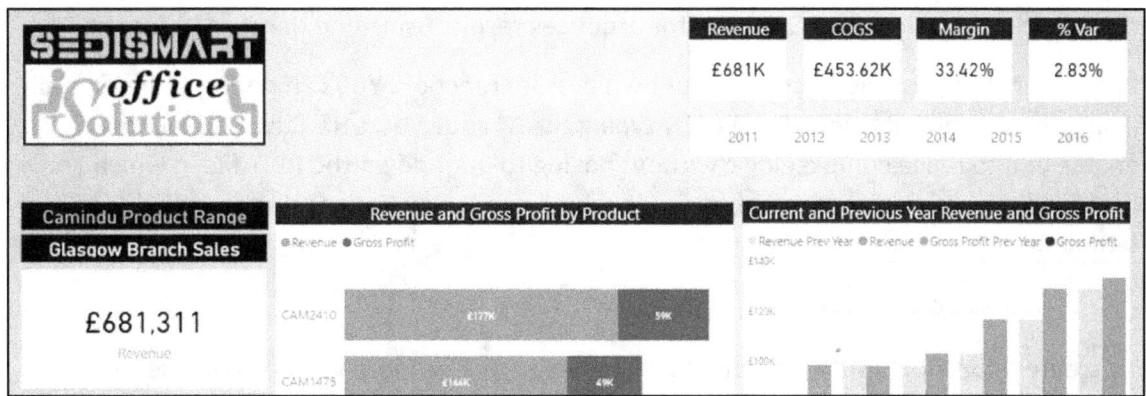

## Conclusion

The combination of templates and parameters provides a great mechanism for streamlining and standardizing report creation.

Parameters allow you to easily make key elements of a report dependent on a series of parameter values.

The data type of parameter values can be specified, and the parameter value can also be selected from a drop-down list.

Templates allow you to export a report definition containing queries, parameters, the report pages and an empty data model.

Users can then repeatedly instantiate the Template using Power BI Desktop. Each time the template is used, the user must supply values for all obligatory parameters. Power BI then creates a new PBIX file using those values.

# Chapter 14. Power Query Custom Functions

Functions are found in every programming and development environment and enable users to perform complex calculations without having to constantly recreate complex algorithms. The M language which underlies the Power Query environment is no exception. Each of the commands available in the Query Editor produces results using one or more M functions.

In addition, it is possible to create your own custom function. You can do this either visually (using the Query Editor interface) or by typing the M code yourself. Custom functions enable you to reuse complex logic without having to hunt down the PBIX file in which you first used that particular series of steps. For this reason, functions are often included in templates.

## Converting a Query to a Function

To create a function visually, you first parameterize one or more values, then use the Convert to Function command. Let us take an example of how we might use a function to speed up our data preparation workflows.

The ability to connect to a folder of data allows you to combine all the files in a given folder into a single table. But, what if you wish to apply that same logic to a series of files in different locations? Ideally, you would want to create a list of files and then use a function to assemble them into a single table.

In the training folder, and in the sub-folder "14-Power Query custom functions", you will find an Excel file called "List.xlsx" which contains the following list of files.

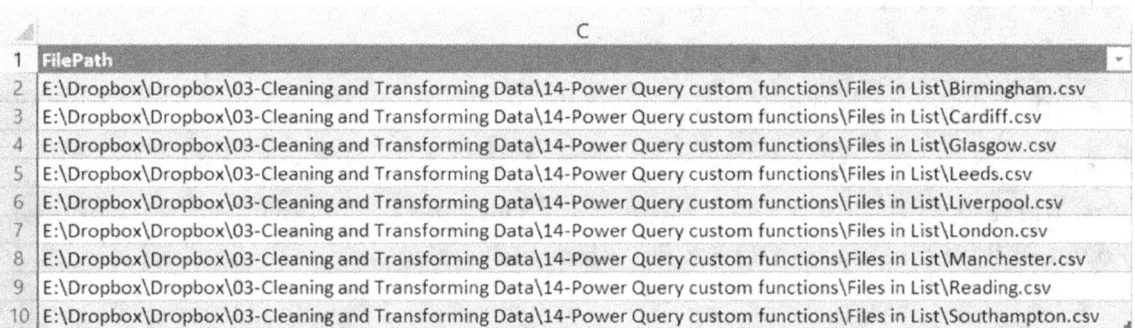

For convenience, all the files are, in fact, in the same folder; however, you will, hopefully, agree that we could also use this technique to list files in a series of disparate locations.

To create our function, we begin by importing a file which has the same structure as the files which we will be combining; specifically, the same column headings. In the "14-Power Query custom functions" folder, we have prepared such a file; it is called "Example.csv". If you open the file in a text editor, or in Excel, you will see that it contains only the column headings.

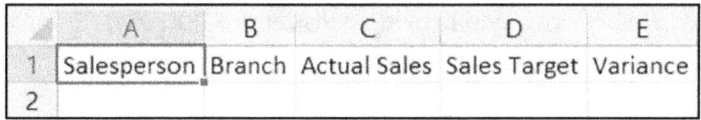

## Connecting to our Example file

Our first step is to connect to the file called "Example.csv", by choosing **Home > Get Date > Text/CSV**.

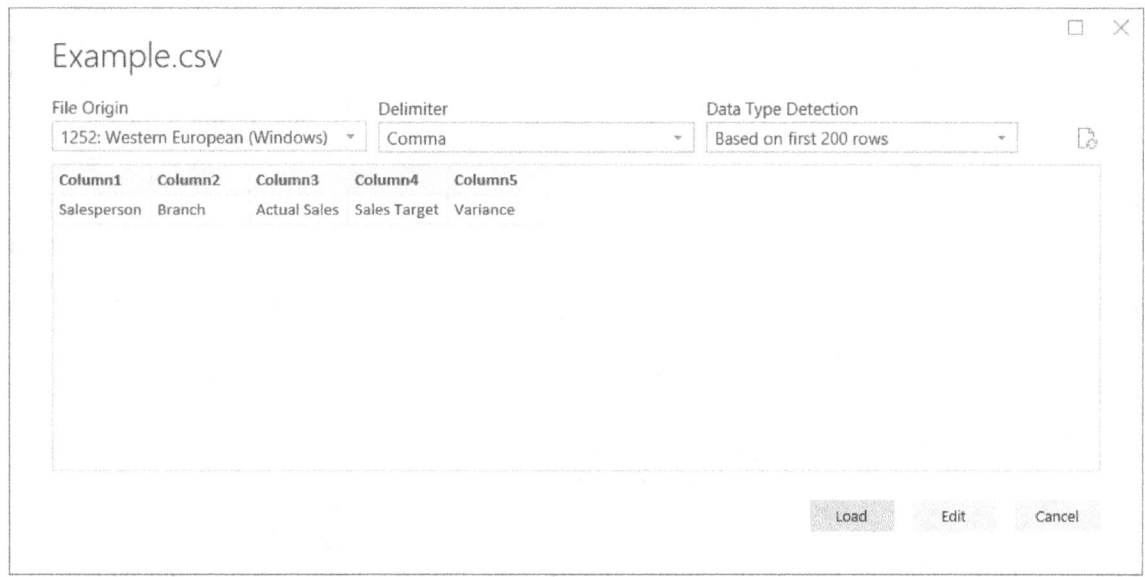

We can see from the preview that the column headers are being treated as data; so, to fix this we need to click on **Edit**, not **Load**. Then, we click on **Home > Transform > Use first Row as Headers**.

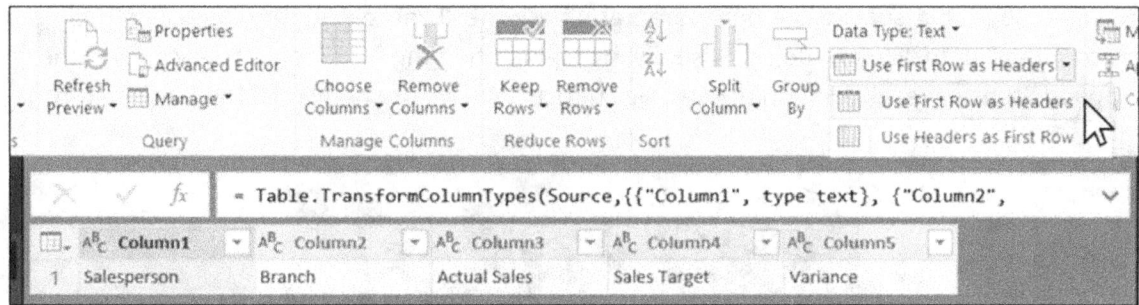

This gives us the basic framework of our function. The next step is to add a parameter.

## Creating a parameter

For any function to be useful (in any environment), it will normally require one or more parameters. Custom M functions are the same; and the parameters feature which we examined in the last chapter can also provide a visual method of defining a function parameter.

Click **Home > Parameters > Manage Parameters > New Parameter**. Enter the name "File Path"; set the **Type** to **Text**; leave the **Suggested Values** set to **Any Value**; and paste in the file path of the "Example.csv" on your own system into the **Current Value** field.

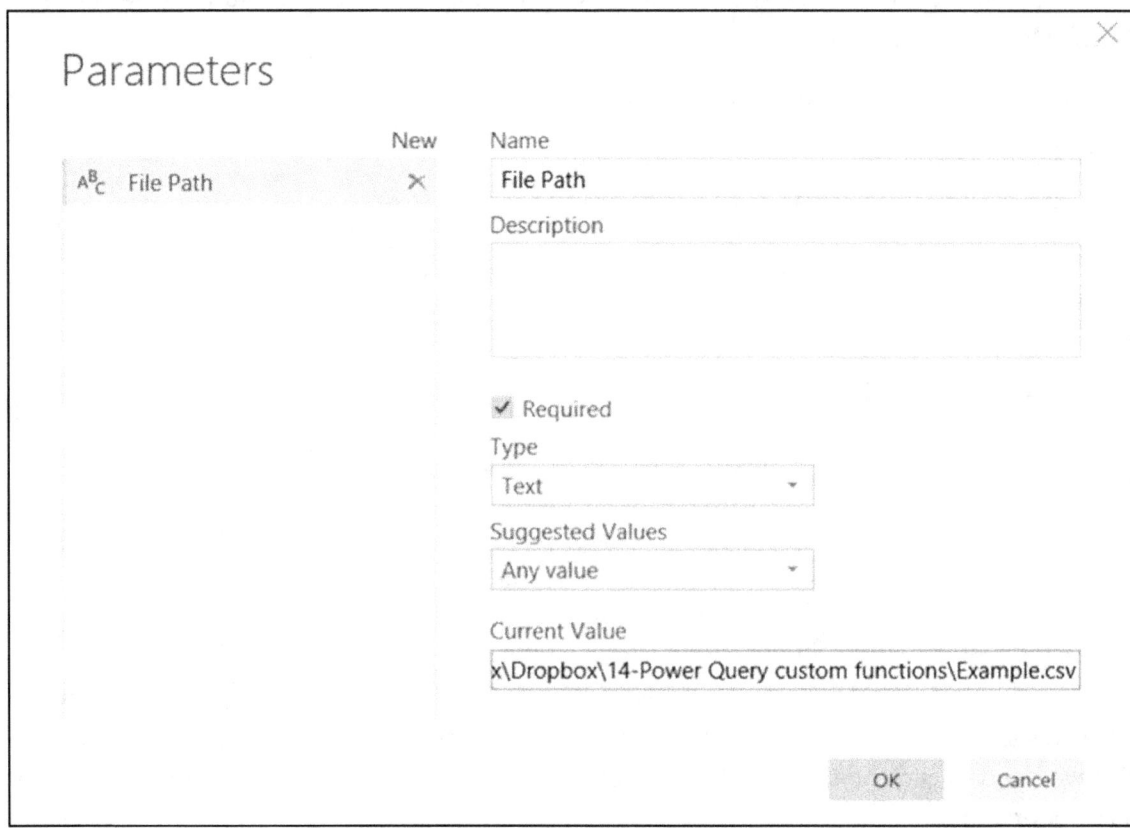

Now we need to associate our new parameter with the "Example" query, replacing the static, literal path. We can do this visually, by highlighting the "Example" query and, in the Applied Steps pane, clicking on the settings button (the cog icon) next to the Source step.

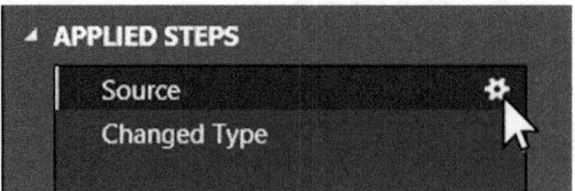

When the Comma-Separated dialog appears, choose **Parameter** from the **File path** drop-down.

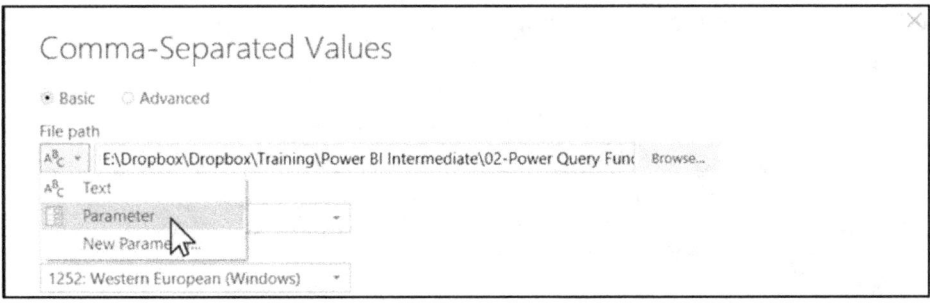

Since we have only created one parameter, called "File Path", it will be automatically selected; so, just click **OK**.

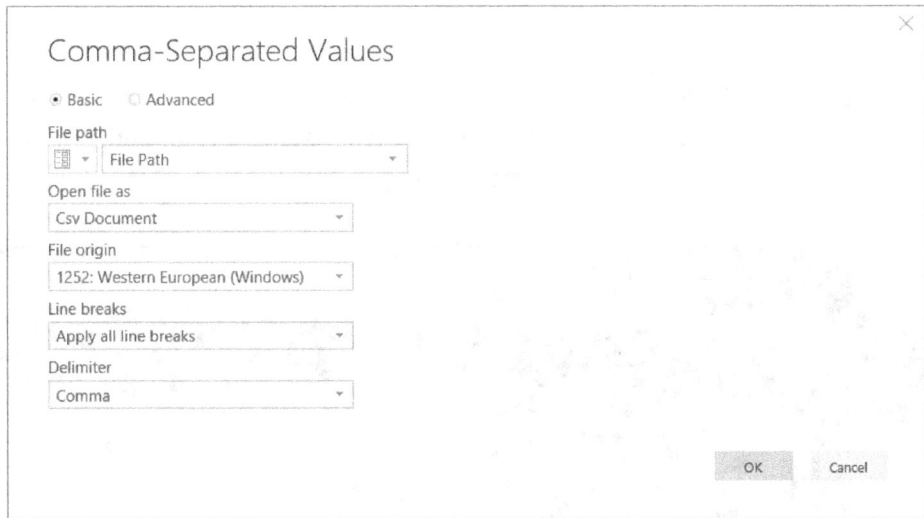

Now that we have associated a parameter with the "Example" query, we can convert it to a function. To do this, right click on the query and choose **Create Function** from the context menu.

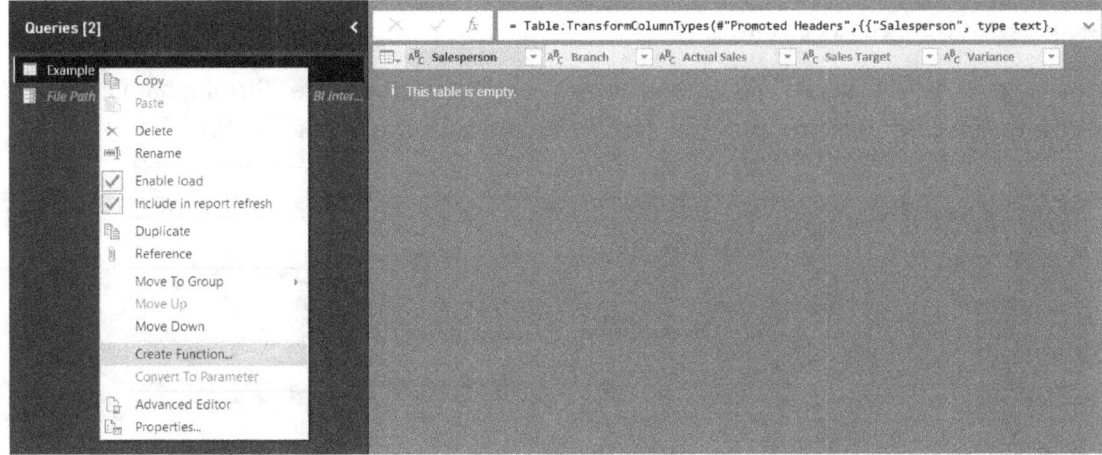

When the Create Function dialog appears, name the function "Import Sales Data" and click **OK**.

In the Queries pane, on the left of the Query Editor interface, Power BI creates a group (a folder) called "Import Sales Data", the same name as our new function; and places inside it the "Example" query, the "File Path" parameter and the "Import Sales Data" function.

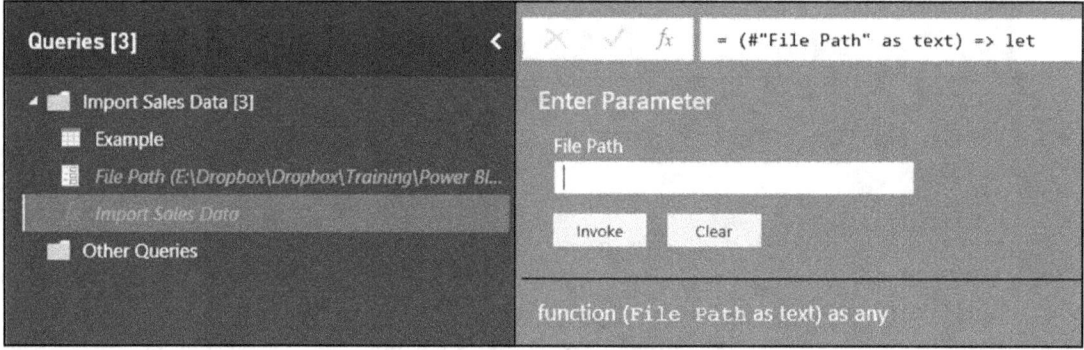

## Invoking a Function

The first method of using a function is to `enter a value for each parameter and then click on the Invoke button. Let's do that.

Navigate to the "Files in List" folder and copy the full path to the file "Birmingham.csv"; paste into the **Enter Parameter > File Path** field; and click the **Invoke** button.

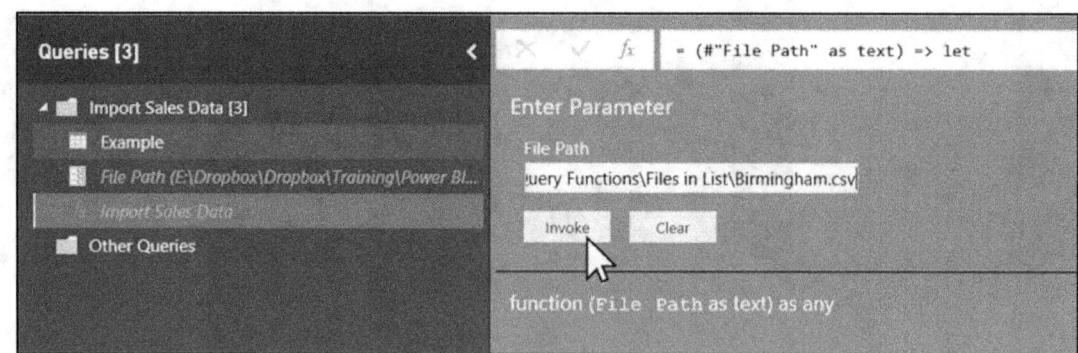

Power BI now creates a new query called "Invoked Function" which is the result of the applying the steps in the function to the file at the location which we entered as the function parameter. Since this file contains data, the "Invoked Function" query retrieves this data.

Invoking a function in this way is useful for testing purposes; but, in this example, it would not save us much time. To combine all the files, we would have to invoke the function repeatedly and then combine the resulting queries using the Append Queries command.

Fortunately, Power BI provides a far more powerful way of deploying our function: the Invoke Custom Function command.

## Using the Invoke Custom Function Command

The Invoke function command allows us to apply a function using the values in one of the columns of a table as the input for a function parameter. The function is applied to each row of the specified column; and the results of the function are stored in a new column which may consist of binary information such as tables.

So, let us now delete the unwanted "Invoked Function" query and import the file called "List.xlsx" in the "02-Power Query Functions" folder. (Click **Home > New Query > New Source > Excel**.) When the Navigator dialog appears, click on the checkbox next to the table called "FileList" and click **OK**.

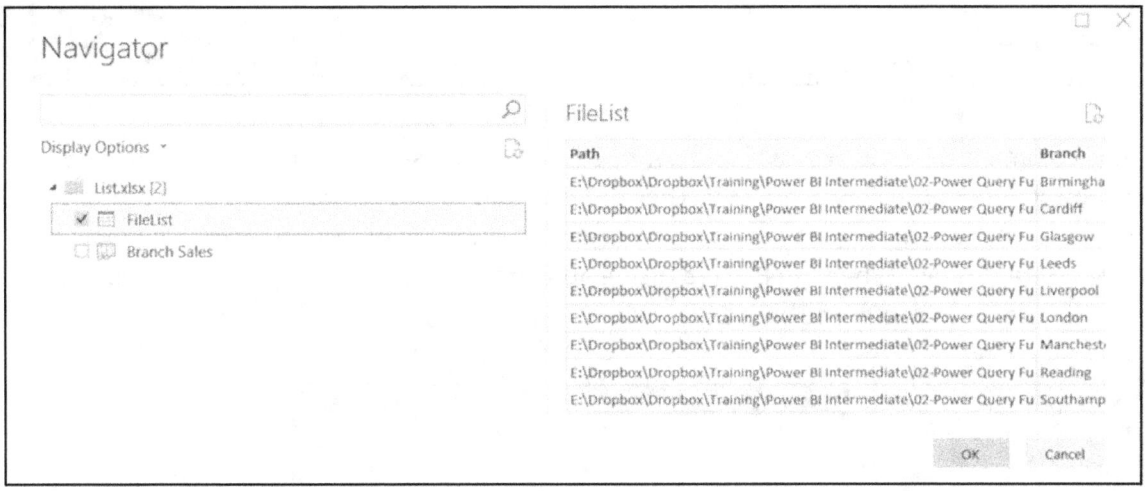

Next, click **Add Column > General > Invoke Custom Column**. In the Invoke Custom Column dialog, leave the default column name in place. Since the "Import Sales Data" function is the only one in our solution, it will automatically be selected as the **Function Query** option. Below this, the list of function parameters contains only one item: File Path. Next to this we have a drop-down containing a list of all the columns in the FileList table; choose FilePath from the list then click **OK**.

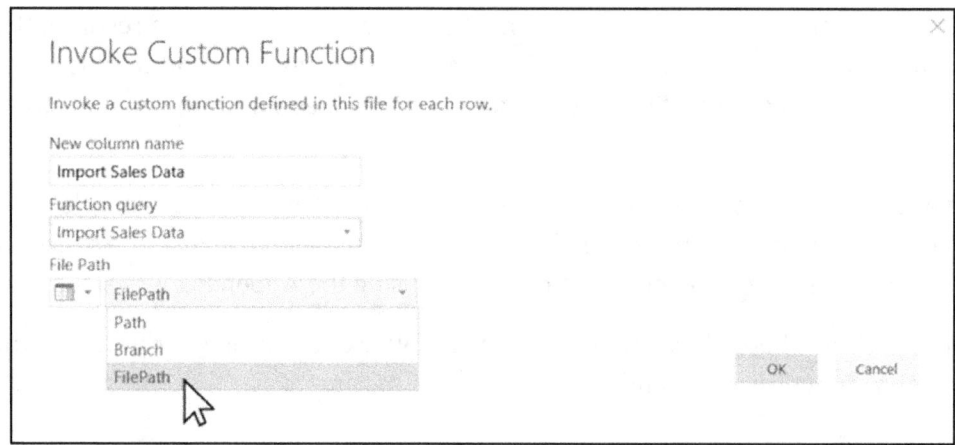

Power BI now creates a new column containing a binary table for each row, based on the value supplied via the FilePath column.

This column is the only one that we now need; so, we can select all the other columns and delete them (**Right-click** > Remove). Then, all we need to do is to expand this column to combine the tables. Click on the Expand button, on the right of the newly-created Import Sales Data column. When the Expand dialog appears, deactivate the option **Use original column name as prefix** and click **OK**.

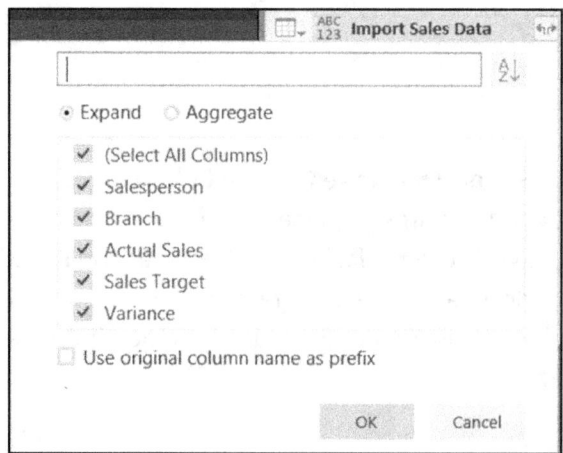

Our "File List" query now expands to include the data in all the files listed in the File Path column. Let us end by renaming the query "Sales All Branches"; and, to verify that the table does, indeed, contain sales data for all branches, click on the filter arrow on the right of the Branch column header.

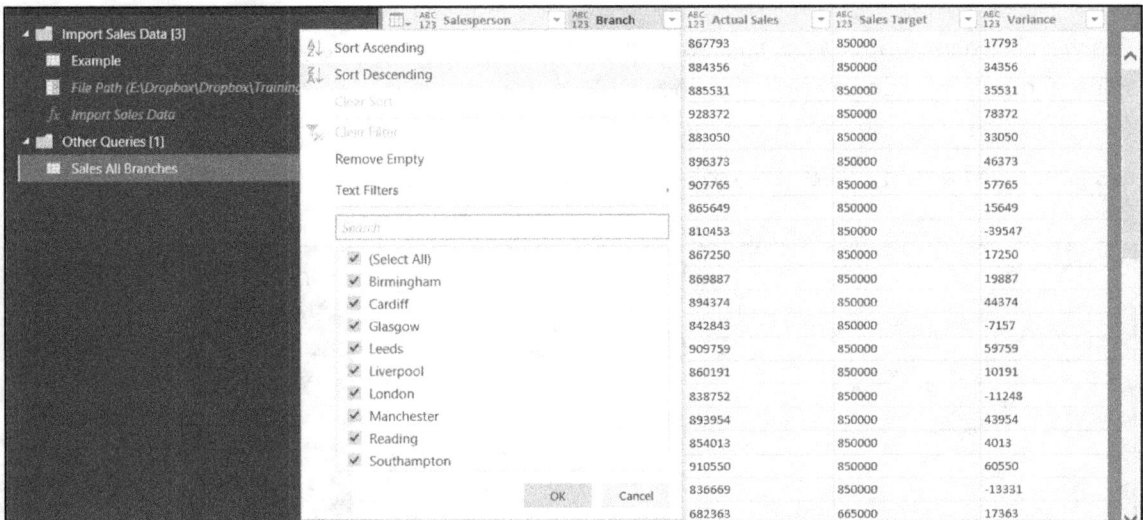

To end this section, click **File > Close & Apply**; save the file as "Convert to Function.pbix"; then close it.

## Understanding Function Syntax

Having looked at creating a function automatically, let us now examine the basic M language syntax for creating a function. To write a function (or any other query) from scratch, in a new Power BI Desktop file, click **Home > Get Data > Blank Query**. Then, to look at the M code behind the query, click **Home > Query > Advanced Editor**.

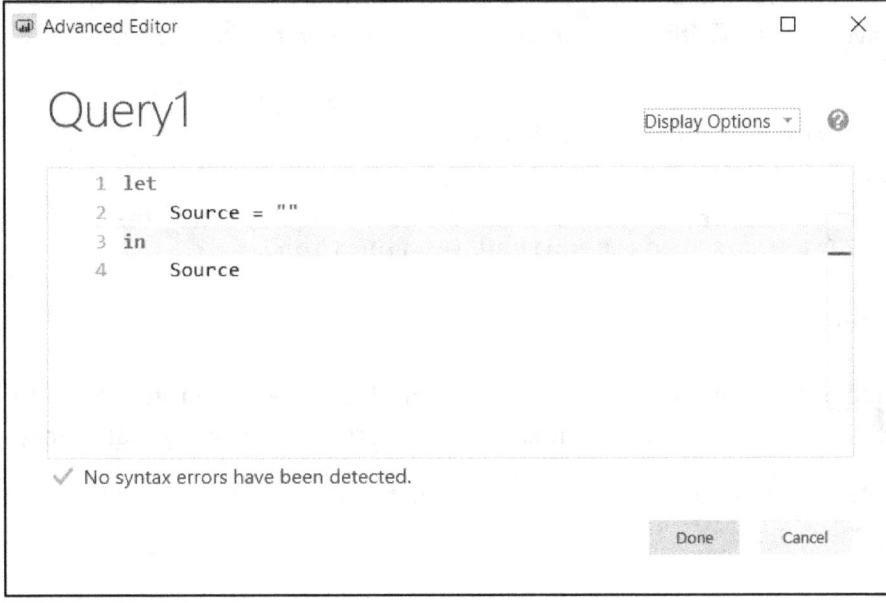

The code you see in the Advanced Editor window consists of a **let ... in** statement block; the classic M structure used in most queries. This code block can contain a series of statements with the following basic structure:

```
Variable1 = Expression
Variable2 = Expression
```

The variable names appear as named steps in the Applied Steps pane. Thus, even in this skeletal query, we can see how the line

```
Source = ""
```

has generated a step called "Source" in the Applied Steps pane.

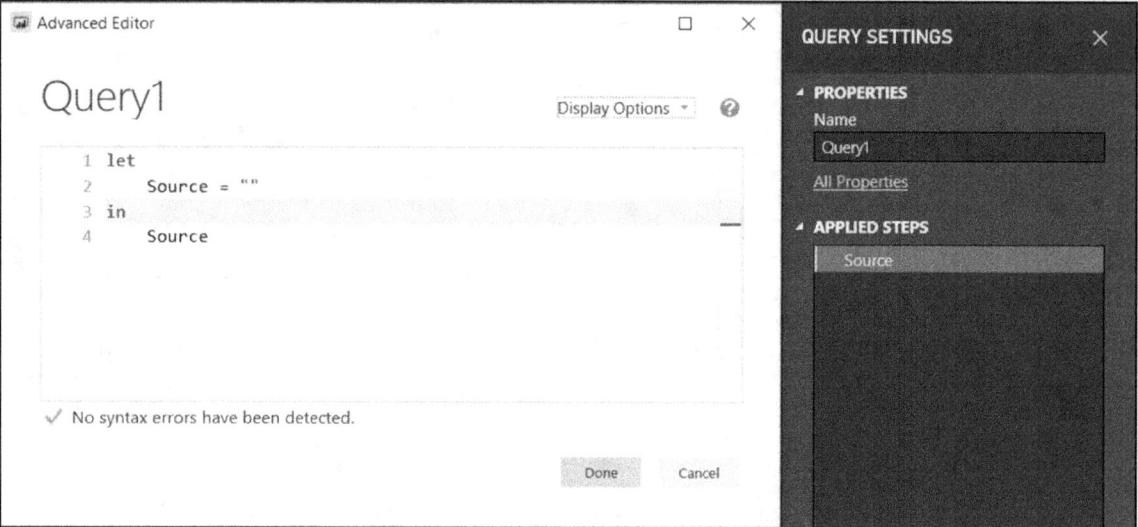

Each line inside a let block, except for the last, must end with a comma. In the blank query code shown above, there is only one line; so, no comma is required.

The expression referenced by the in statement is returned as the result of the query; and, when we have finished writing our function, will determine the value returned by the function.

The basic syntax of an M function is as follows.

```
let
    MyFunction = (Param1 as ParamType[,…]) as ResultType =>
    // Expressions required by function
in
    MyFunction
```

The definition of the function is placed inside a variable (here given the generic name "MyFunction"); then, the in statement is used to return (the result of) that function.

The parameter(s) required by the function as its input(s) are placed inside parentheses followed by the symbol **=>**.

To specify the data type of each parameter, we use the **as** keyword. Immediately following the parentheses, we use the **as** keyword again, in a statement which specifies the data type returned by the function.

Then, we have the expressions required to calculate the function result. And, finally, we use the in statement to return a value.

## Creating a Date of Birth function

Let us take a slightly more challenging example. This time, we will write an M function, from scratch, which will calculate a person's age based on their date of birth, as listed in a column called "DOB".

Create a blank query; then, click **Home > Query > Advanced Editor** and replace the default code with the M code shown below.

```
let
    Age = (DOB as date) as number =>
        if
            DOB < #date(
                Date.Year (DOB),
                Date.Month(DateTime.LocalNow()),
                Date.Day(DateTime.LocalNow())
                )
        then
            Date.Year(DateTime.LocalNow()) - Date.Year (DOB) -
1
        else
            Date.Year(DateTime.LocalNow()) - Date.Year (DOB)
    in
        Age
```

Here, we define a single date parameter for our Age function: DOB. We also specify that the function will return a number. Then we have the **=>** symbol, followed by an **if** statement.

In M, **if** statements have the following generic format:

```
If LogicalTest then expression(s) else expression(s)
```

There are no parentheses and no **end if** statement. Here, our logical test checks to see whether the value passed via the DOB parameter is less than a date which uses the year of the current date and the month and day of the DOB parameter value.

If the test is true, then we subtract the year of the DOB parameter value from the year of the current date; then, we subtract and extra 1 year, since the person has not yet had their birthday.

Otherwise, we simply subtract the year of the DOB parameter value from the year of the current date.

We end the code by returning the value of the Age variable as the result of the function.

Rename the new function "Age".

Let us now import the data which we will use to test our function. In the Query Editor, click on **Home > New Source > Excel** and navigate to the file "14-Power Query custom functions\Patient Data.xlsx". Import the single worksheet which the file contains: "Contacts".

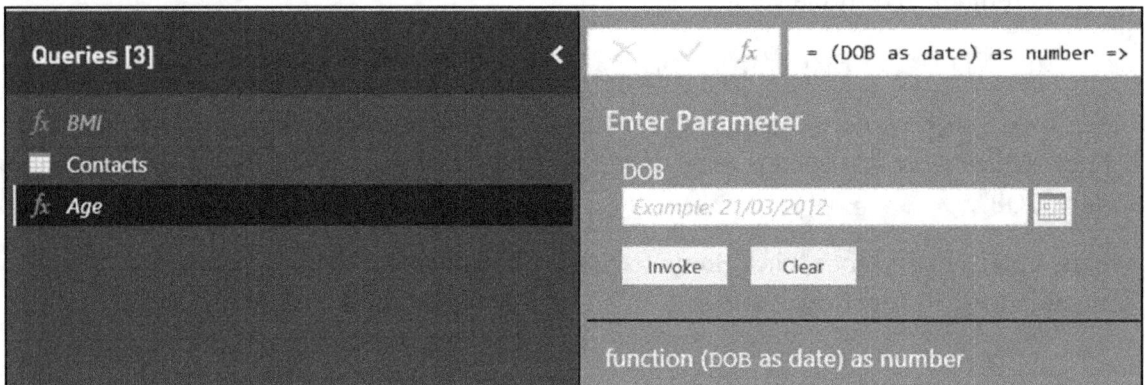

To add an Age column to the imported table, highlight the "Contacts" query and click **Add Column > General > Invoke Custom Function**.

In the Invoke Custom Function dialog, enter the function name "Age" and choose the **Age** function from the **Function query** drop-down. Set the **DOB** parameter to **Column Name > DOB** and click **OK**.

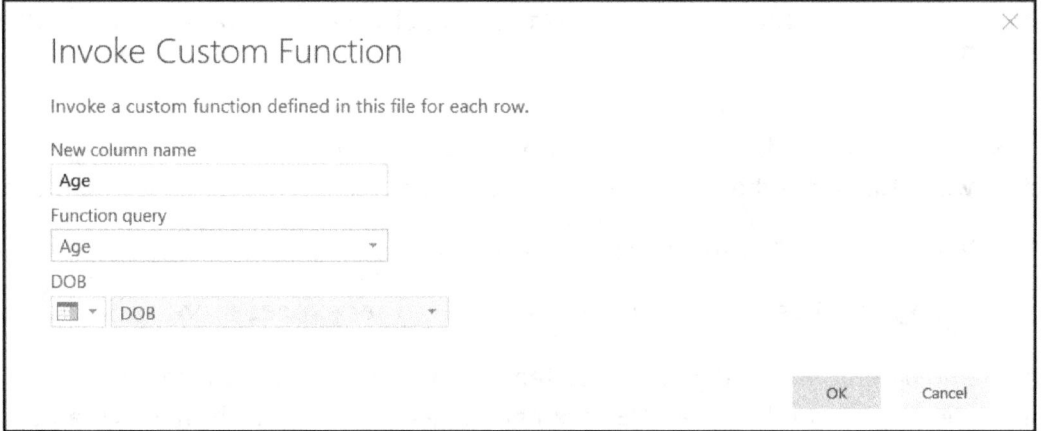

A new column called Age is generated and containing a numeric value for each row. This time, we need to change the column type to **Whole Number**.

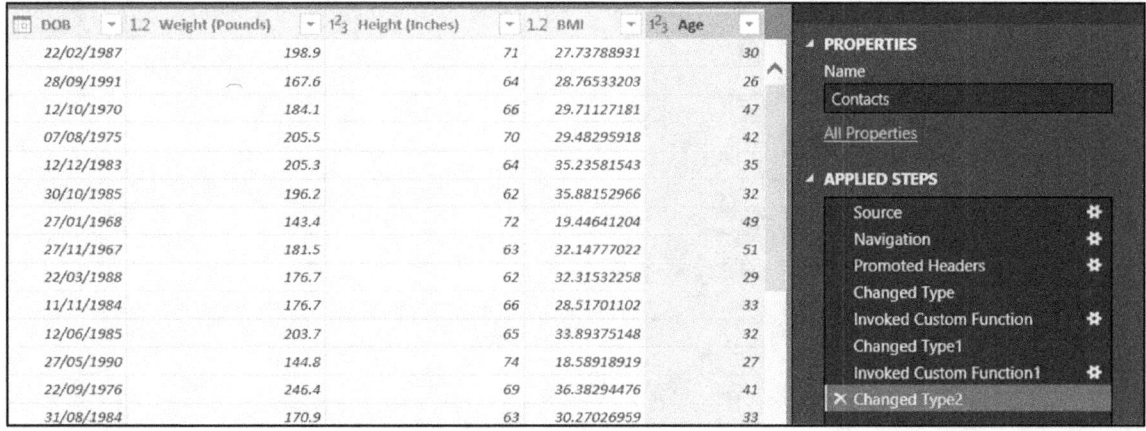

Click **File > Close & Apply**; save the file as "Writing an M Function.pbix"; then close the file.

## Conclusion

Power Query custom functions allow you to create reusable and flexible queries which produce consistent results.

Custom functions can be created automatically in the Query Editor, by **Right-click**ing a query and choosing **Convert to Function**.

To be useful, a custom function will normally require at least one parameter.

The **Add Column > General > Invoke Custom Column** command provides the most powerful visual method of running a custom function.